101
RULES
OF
THUMB

For Low Energy Architecture

To Betty

My gratitude is due to Tod Wakefield, Head of School at Portsmouth School of Architecture, for his encouragement and advice throughout the process of creating this book. The lack of rules of thumb was identified, in the UK conference series 'Designs on the Planet,' as a hindrance to educators and practitioners. Subsequently, the Centre for Education in the Built Environment (CEBE) published a case study of mine, which was a precursor to this book, and I am grateful to Andy Roberts and CEBE.

Many educators, practitioners, colleagues and clients have been an influence over the years and some of these are: Andy Ford; Professor Edward Ng, who introduced me to Dean Hawkes, Baruch Givoni and Brian Edwards; Brendan Redican; colleagues and students at the University of Portsmouth School of Architecture and staff at the University Library. The thoughts of my own teachers, who threw light on the subject in my formative years, remain in my mind.

The book would not yet have seen the light of day without the assistance of James Scrace.

I am grateful to RIBA Publishing, and to James Thompson, who immediately saw the point of the book and enthusiastically set about making it real.

I thank my wife Betty for her steadfast support, as well as Anna and Nick for their confidence in what they insisted on calling my book.

RIBA ⧉ **Publishing**

© Huw Heywood, 2012

Published by RIBA Publishing, 66 Portland Place, London W1B 1AD

ISBN 987 1 85946 481 6

Stock code 78992

Reprinted 2014/2019

The right of Huw Heywood to be identified as the Author of this Work has been asserted in accordance with the Copyright, Design and Patents Act 1988.

British Library Cataloguing in Publications Data

A catalogue record for this book is available from the British Library.

Commissioning Editor: James Thompson

Production: Kate Mackillop

Designed and typeset by Luis Peral-Aranda

Printed and bound by W & G Baird Limited, Northern Ireland

RIBA Publishing is part of RIBA Enterprises Ltd.

www.ribaenterprises.com

HUW HEYWOOD

101

RULES

OF

THUMB

For Low Energy Architecture

CONTENTS

PREFACE

Throughout history, people have constructed buildings with an intuitive responsiveness towards the environment and the climate in which they live, ensuring their own comfort while respecting limited resources and working with, not against, the forces of nature. By returning to an understanding of the basic principles involved in the ways that buildings respond to their surroundings, we can significantly reduce energy needs. Guidance on how to design buildings that need little or no energy for heating, lighting and cooling is the specific focus of this book.

We use energy to heat, light and cool our buildings. Much of the energy we use is derived from fossil fuels (oil, coal, gas), which are finite global resources. They will eventually run out. Before we seek to replace this fossil-fuel-derived energy with renewable or alternative energy sources (sun, wind, water or plant-based), we should first aim to ensure that our buildings use as little energy as possible, irrespective of where that energy comes from. Any energy source will result, from its production, supply and use, in negative impacts on the planet.

Aside from fossil fuels being a finite resource, there is a second reason to reduce the amount of energy used in our buildings. The way in which we convert fossil fuels into the energy we use for heat, light and power results in the generation of carbon dioxide (CO_2), one of the greenhouse gases. A link has therefore been made between buildings, global warming and climate change. In fact, buildings are responsible for nearly half of all the CO_2 emissions we generate.

Certainly energy is used in the construction of buildings – for example, from the mechanical excavation of clay to its firing and then the transportation of the resulting brick to the construction site – and this is a serious issue for designers to tackle. But by far the most energy is used by buildings during their lifetime. All of us who commission, design, operate and inhabit buildings therefore have a significant role, and a responsibility, in reducing the energy used in the operation of our buildings.

INTRODUCTION, AND WHAT THE RULES OF THUMB ARE FOR

Our ancestors knew how to create comfortable indoor conditions with modest use of resources in their indigenous architecture and we must now re-learn their intuitive skills and apply them for tomorrow's world. This book seeks to reintroduce to the reader that intuitive knowledge, explaining what works in buildings which use little or no energy in their operation, wherever they happen to be on the planet. It aims to provide the reader with two things:

- An understanding of the universal rules of nature which govern the way buildings respond to their environment, and

- Specific low energy-use, rule-of-thumb solutions for new buildings or for retrofitting existing buildings

The rules of thumb are about the fundamentals of energy efficiency. For those who wish to proceed into measurement, calculation, modelling and further research, a narrative bibliography provides guidance on the key texts and some of the basic formulae which lie behind the rules.

Buildings exist to modify the climate, from whatever the outside conditions might be, to create a comfortable indoor environment. For new buildings the process by which this is achieved is an integrated one which starts with consideration of the siting and location of a building, moves to deliberations on orientation and form and then on to the design of the building envelope (the walls, roof and floor, also known as the building fabric in this book) and to the interior spaces. The final stage is one in which the occupants decide whether their building has succeeded in creating a comfortable environment and if not they make themselves comfortable, traditionally by using energy to supply heating or cooling. It is the need for the use of energy which the rules of thumb seek to limit.

The design process described above is reflected in the organisation of this book. It is worth noting that the early design decisions are more permanent than the later ones: for example, unless the result is a transportable architecture, the location and orientation of a building will not change once the building is built, whereas the building envelope can be upgraded with additional insulation, or in response to new technologies which become available. The early architectural considerations have a major bearing on the energy efficiency of a building. The decisions are crucial, and so had better be right: the rules of thumb are there to provide guidance on these early, permanent moves which link our buildings with the natural world and which are also key ingredients of a poetic architecture.

The book aims to be relevant globally, which presents a number of challenges to author and reader. One difficulty all design teachers face is how to refer to where the sun is, a fundamental factor influencing many of the rules of thumb. When referring to the façade of a building which is oriented towards the midday sun the term 'south-facing' is fine in the northern hemisphere, but in the southern hemisphere it traverses the sky in the north, so the façade facing the sun is north-facing. I have opted mainly to use the awkward, but functional, 'solar-oriented' or 'south-facing (north in the southern hemisphere)' and, occasionally, 'equator-facing'. The façade opposite the sun is sometimes referred to, again rather clumsily, as 'non-solar-oriented'. Hemisphere-centric terms are used only where the term is a well known maxim.

Finally, a brief glimpse of the future, in which buildings will need to be more resilient and adaptable to an unpredictable climate. The rules of thumb are applicable to today's climate regions and to future uncertainties. For example, some temperate regions might experience climates more like the hot-summer/cold-winter climates discussed in the book, meaning that the rules which apply today in winter in cold regions and in summer in hot regions will need to be considered. Through their simplicity, the rules of thumb invite creativity in making low energy-use buildings and cities which are both delightful and responsive to human needs in an ever-changing world.

CHAPTER 1
WORKING WITH SITE AND LOCATION

- Sun and shade
- Climate and micro-climate
- Shelter from wind and rain

1. BUILDINGS USE HALF THE WORLD'S ENERGY

We use half of all the energy we generate in the world, much of which is created by the burning of fossil fuels, to run our buildings. Add transport to and from those buildings, and designers of the built environment have some control over, and responsibility for, 75% of global energy use.

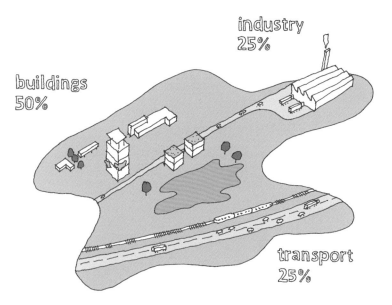

industry
25%

buildings
50%

transport
25%

2. THINK BEFORE YOU BUILD

Buildings last an age and consume energy throughout their lives, so whether to build or not to build is a big question. The answer might be to refurbish, reorganise, change business strategy or change your life rather than to build something new, and this might be the lowest long-term energy-use solution. Consider all options.

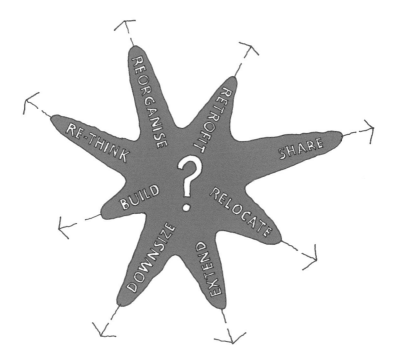

3. THE SUN RISES IN THE EAST AND SETS IN THE WEST

It is worth reminding ourselves of this most basic rule. However, it is also worth remembering that, even outside the equatorial regions, in the mid-latitudes of the northern hemisphere winter the sun rises south of east and in the summer it rises north of east. This means that in summer the north face of a building in these regions might be very briefly exposed to the sun, but in the winter the sun will never warm that building's northern face. In the northern hemisphere, after rising, the sun will be seen traversing across the sky in the south. The reverse is true south of the equator.

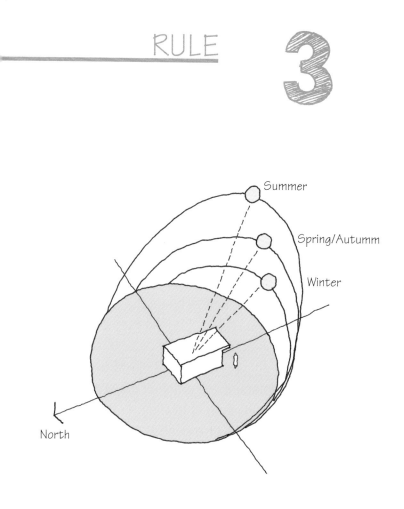

Summer

Spring/Autumm

Winter

North

4. THE HEIGHT OF THE SUN ABOVE THE HORIZON DETERMINES MANY ASPECTS OF A CLIMATE-RESPONSIVE ARCHITECTURE

In December the highest altitude of the sun above the horizon at midday in London is around 15°. This angle varies according to latitude, and that is part of what makes every individual location on earth unique. The diagram gives December sun angles for cities around the world. Using sun-path diagrams or simple-to-use web-based calculators, the position of the sun at any time of day or any time of the year can be found out. Knowing the relative position of earth and sun, or solar geometry, is an important aspect of climate-responsive architecture.

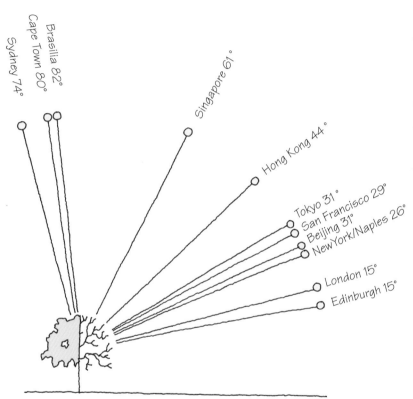

Sydney 74°
Cape Town 80°
Brasilia 82°
Singapore 61°
Hong Kong 44°
Tokyo 31°
San Francisco 29°
Beijing 31°
New York/Naples 26°
London 15°
Edinburgh 15°

21 December - The angle of the sun at midday
at different places on the planet

5. THE SUN'S RAYS TURN TO HEAT ON CONTACT WITH ANY SURFACE

The way this happens is rooted in quantum mechanics, but the simple result is that the earth, and everything on it, is warmed by the sun, making all life possible. The heating of the earth also results in climate and weather, which vary greatly depending upon where we are on the planet.

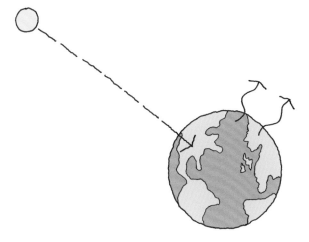

6. IF YOU DO NOT WANT HEAT INSIDE, KEEP THE SUN OUT

Just as the earth is warmed by the sun, so is any other surface that the sun's rays reach. This is an important rule because if you are trying to avoid overheating in a building you must prevent direct sunlight from entering: once direct sunlight has entered a building, it's too late to stop it becoming heat.

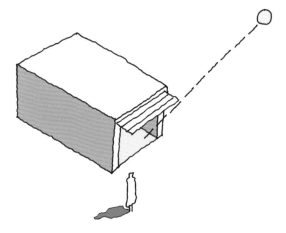

7. HARNESS THE POWER OF THE LOW WINTER SUN – IT IS A FREE SOURCE OF HEAT

In the winter the sun is low in the sky, so the sun can penetrate deep into a space, if it is allowed to, bringing free heat with it.

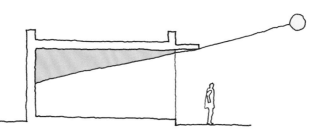

8. PREVENT OVERHEATING IN SUMMER

In the summer the sun is high in the sky, reaching, in June, a maximum angle of about 62° above the horizon in London, 73° in both Beijing and New York, and 83° in Cairo. In Sydney in December the sun reaches about 80° above the horizon. For solar-oriented windows a simple, external horizontal shading device can prevent this high-angle summer sun from entering a building. Rule-of-thumb depths of projection from near the head of a window are: 600–900mm deep in the mid-latitudes; and at least 1,200mm deep close to the equator, where a combination of vertical and horizontal projections should be employed.

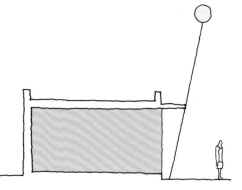

9. SITE TOPOGRAPHY INFORMS US ABOUT BUILDING LOCATION

Topography, the form of the land, must be studied before you begin to design. Wind direction and intensity are affected by hills, valleys and other natural features. Often, in valleys and mountainous terrain the wind patterns change between day and night. The direction of the wind might be read in the direction in which grasses have been blown on a site.

10. A WINDBREAK WILL HALVE THE WIND SPEED AND LEAD TO REDUCED COOLING OF THE BUILDING ENVELOPE

A windbreak, or shelter belt, will significantly influence the wind. Locating a building on the leeward side of a well-designed windbreak can result in energy savings of 15 to 20% because cooling of the building envelope is reduced. Position the building within five times the height of the windbreak. Remember: you will want to permit, not block, the passage of breezes in tropical regions.

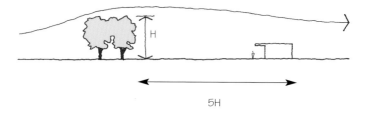

5H

11. THE WIND SPEED WILL BE INFLUENCED AT A GREAT DISTANCE FROM A WINDBREAK

The wind's velocity will be reduced up to around 20 times the height of the windbreak, so even distant shelter belts will contribute to reduced energy use.

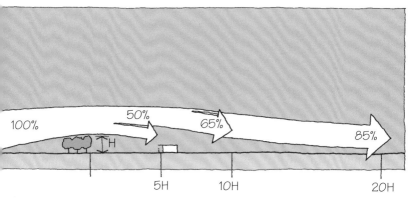

12. THE PRESENCE OF WATER IS A FREE SOURCE OF COOLING

A body of water, such as a lake or the sea, will influence air temperature and humidity. Water that has been exposed to the night sky in summer will cool the breeze that passes over it during warm days. Site a building such that water-cooled breezes can be directed into it. Daytime onshore sea breezes should be put to use by orienting buildings towards the sea in humid and warm climates and seasons.

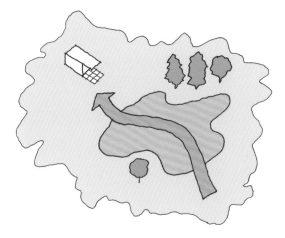

13. **AVOID OVERSHADOWING IN WINTER, AS THIS WILL COOL THE BUILDING ENVELOPE**

The envelope of a building must be kept warm in cooler climates and seasons. If it is in shade, more energy will be needed to achieve comfortable thermal conditions within.

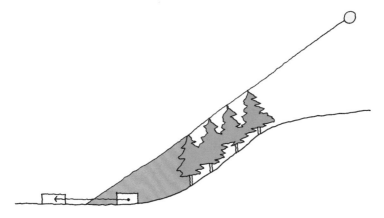

Move out of shade

14. TREES CAN PROVIDE SUMMER SHADING AND ALLOW WINTER SOLAR GAINS

Trees can be useful shading devices. Deciduous trees can block up to 85% of the sun's radiation in summer. In winter, without leaves, they permit up to 70% of the sun's energy to pass between their bare branches. However, it would take a very large tree to almost fully shade a solar-oriented façade in summer, and proximity to trees and tree roots might bring other problems for both building and tree. A compromise rule of thumb is to position the tree such that the canopy sits outside a line drawn at 45° from the base of the building, as indicated in the lower diagram.

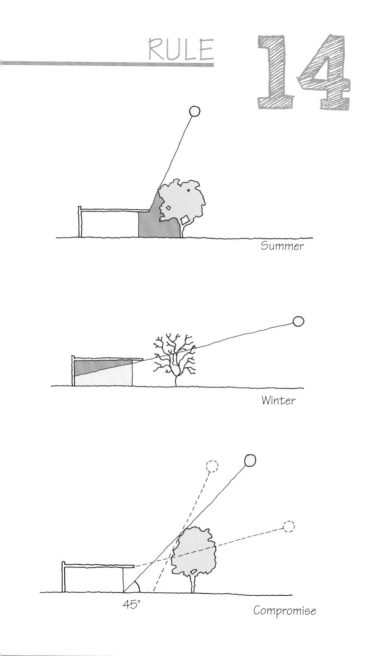

Summer

Winter

45°

Compromise

15. USE LANDSCAPE FOR FREE SUMMER COOLING

Planting can be used not only to divert the path of the wind but also to assist in the cooling of breezes. The ground shaded by a tree or other planting will be cooler than the surrounding areas, and so warm breezes will be cooled as they pass over the shaded ground. The rule is applicable in both urban and rural situations.

16. PROVIDE SHELTER FROM WIND AND RAIN

Wind and rain reduce the temperature of the building envelope, leading to the need for additional energy to heat the interior in cool climates and seasons. Roof overhangs can provide protection from rain. Windbreaks can take a number of forms, all of which can become architectural devices in a design:

- Trees
- Hedges
- Fences
- Garden walls
- Courtyards

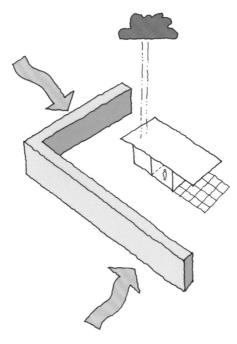

17. BUILT FORM CAN BE USED FOR WIND PROTECTION

Surrounding buildings and walls can be effectively employed as windbreaks. Unlike many large modern cities, medieval town plans and those of mountain villages that are subject to extreme winds do not have a regular grid of streets through which wind has unobstructed access. The direct passage of the wind is impeded by using built form as a barrier.

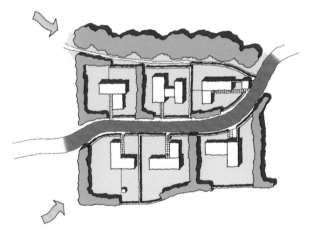

18. A WESTERN TREE BELT CAN PROVIDE SHADE FROM THE LATE AFTERNOON SUN

A carefully positioned tree belt on the western boundaries of a building can give protection from the significant heat of the late-afternoon summer sun. Care needs to be taken to ensure that the winter sun's beneficial heat is not also blocked if working in temperate and cold climate zones. An eastern tree belt will also be beneficial in hot climates, where the morning sun is a powerful force.

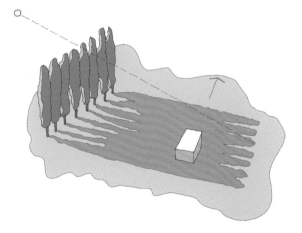

19. 'CLIMATE IS WHAT YOU EXPECT, WEATHER IS WHAT YOU GET'

Sci-fi author Robert Heinlein brought us this useful rule. The weather in Paris might be unseasonably cold with snow storms approaching, but the climate is temperate. Weather, which exists in the thin weather layer surrounding the earth, is a measure of the atmosphere at a particular time. Climate relates to the condition of the atmosphere over a long period of time. Both must be studied in order to know the conditions a building needs to respond to.

CHAPTER 2
MANIPULATING ORIENTATION AND FORM

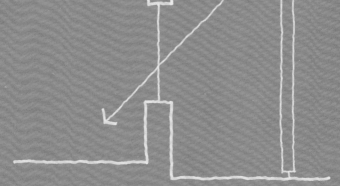

- The relationship between sun and wind

- The impact of building form

20. LEARN FROM THE LOCALS

Indigenous, or vernacular, architecture tends to provide thermal comfort using limited, local resources and energy. Lessons may be learned from both the past and the present where populations live modestly, in tune with their climate and region. Always consider the local vernacular for clues about how buildings perform.

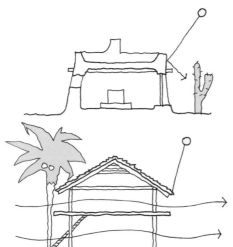

Hot-dry

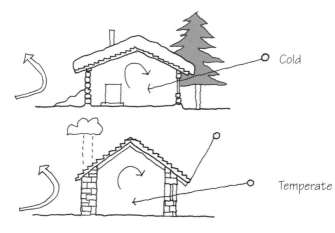

Hot-humid

Cold

Temperate

21. WORK WITH, NOT AGAINST, THE FORCES OF NATURE

Understanding and harnessing the forces of nature in buildings is key to a climate-responsive architecture. The earth is tilted on its axis, bringing us seasons, and its spin influences the winds. The impacts of sun and wind on a place will result from a combination of latitude and altitude, and proximity to sea, mountain or desert. Remember, June is summer in New York and winter in Sydney.

RULE

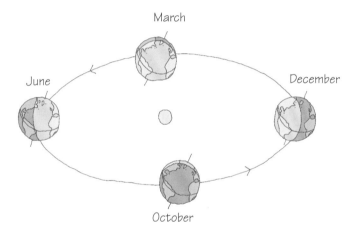

March

June

December

October

22. THE SUN'S STRENGTH VARIES AROUND THE PLANET

Within around 15° of the equator, overheating is the dominant climate-related concern. Here, the east and west elevations of a building are subject to the greatest solar heat gains and winter heating is only an issue at altitude. Outside this band, the solar-oriented façade (south-facing in the northern hemisphere, north-facing in the southern hemisphere) receives the most solar radiation, which may be used for free winter heating but which also may result in unwanted heat gains, leading to overheating in summer.

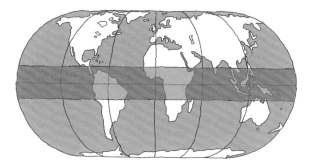

23. GLOBAL AIR MOVEMENTS HAVE A PATTERN

Driven by the sun's variable heating of the earth, and influenced by the motion of the planet, global air movements follow a pattern. The equatorial overheating issue discussed in rule number 22 provides a good example of the relationship between sun and wind: within about 15° of the equator windows should be minimised on east and west façades to avoid heat gains, but the easterly trade winds make ventilation desirable, so well-designed, shaded openings are a good solution in these climate zones.

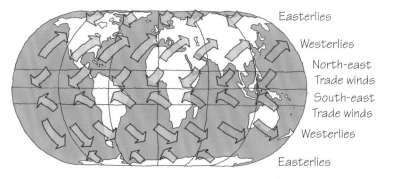

Easterlies

Westerlies

North-east
Trade winds

South-east
Trade winds

Westerlies

Easterlies

24. PUT SUN AND WIND TOGETHER

The position and direction of sun and wind vary season by season. Knowing the relationship between these two powerful forces allows the designer to manipulate a building's orientation and form, the location of its spaces and the position, size and design of openings in order to take advantage of free heating, cooling and ventilation. For example, if in a northern-hemisphere climate the summer winds are southerly (from the south) then south-facing openings can provide cooling ventilation without heat gain as long as they are shaded from the sun.

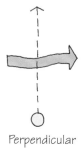

Perpendicular   Coincident   Opposite

25. THE WIND INFLUENCES ENERGY USE

Although global air movements follow a pattern, winds, influenced by weather systems, are very varied. For any given location the amount of time the wind blows from different directions, and its strength and temperature during those times are important factors for low energy building design. The prevailing winds might be said to be south-westerlies, but the strongest or coldest might be easterlies. Knowing the monthly variations by examining historical wind data allows us to plan a building in response.

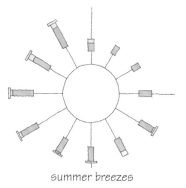

summer breezes

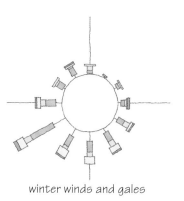

winter winds and gales

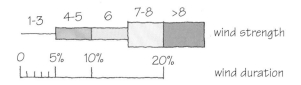

1-3   4-5   6   7-8   >8   wind strength

0   5%   10%   20%   wind duration

26. 'COLD ROOMS TO NORTH, WARM ROOMS TO SOUTH' – CREATE A BUFFER ZONE

It is wise to plan a building such that rooms that require little or no heating or that are occupied only occasionally (such as bedrooms, toilets, store rooms) and rooms that generate their own heat (kitchens, office spaces) are located on the non-solar-oriented face as a buffer zone. The non-solar-oriented face receives little or no sun and may be subject to cold winter winds. Warm rooms, such as living spaces, should face the sun. This rule relates to the architectural idea of 'servant and served' spaces – servant spaces such as kitchens, bathrooms, store rooms and toilets provide a useful buffer for living rooms and other, more frequently inhabited, rooms.

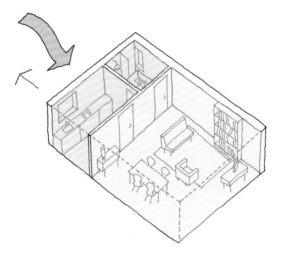

27. THE MAIN FAÇADE SHOULD FACE THE SUN

The main façade of a building should be solar-oriented (or at least within 30° of south in the northern hemisphere, or within 30° of north if you are south of the equator), as this is the easiest orientation to protect from unwanted solar gains in summer – a simple horizontal projection will be effective – and is also the best orientation for capturing free heating in the winter.

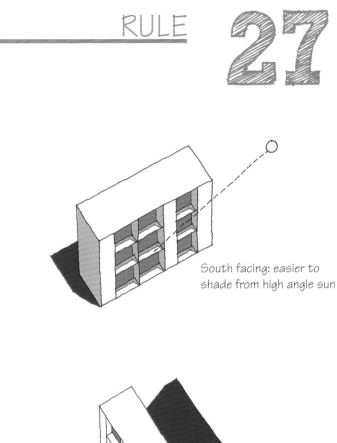

South facing: easier to shade from high angle sun

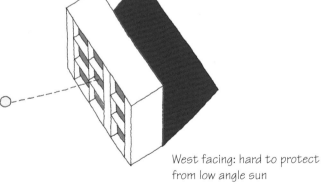

West facing: hard to protect from low angle sun

28. THE SUN IS LOW IN THE SKY IN THE EAST AND THE WEST

It is not just the high angle of the midday sun that can bring unwanted solar gains. In the morning and evening the sun is low in the sky in the east and west respectively, and will bring heat gains to the east and west façades too. The west-facing façade is exposed to a long duration of low-angle, intense solar gain in many climate regions. The low, wide angle of the incident sun on east and west façades therefore presents a different problem to the high angle of the midday sun. Remember, though, that in some locations and seasons the warmth of the early morning sun might be a friendly force of nature, to be harnessed as a means of preheating our habitable spaces at the cold start of the day.

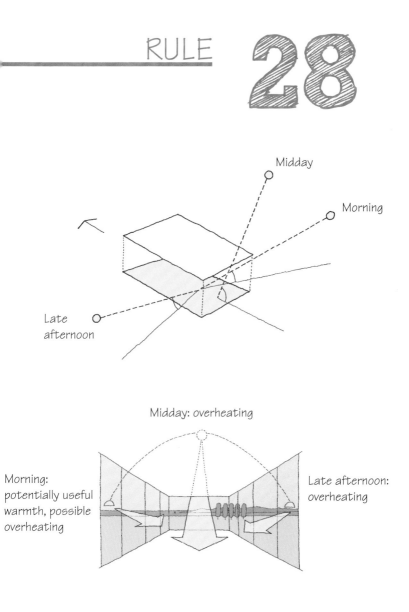

Midday

Morning

Late afternoon

Midday: overheating

Morning: potentially useful warmth, possible overheating

Late afternoon: overheating

29. SUMMER SHADING – SOLUTIONS FOR SOLAR-ORIENTED FAÇADES

The designer has a range of solutions to choose from when considering how to reduce or eliminate the potential for unwanted solar gains. Use external, not internal, shading devices as this prevents the sun's rays from entering the building. Some solutions are:

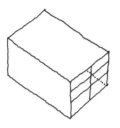

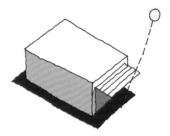

1. Horizontal brise soleil

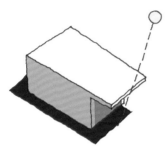

2. Roof overhang

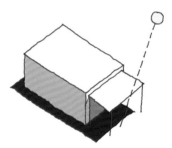

3. Pergola

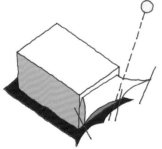

4. Awning

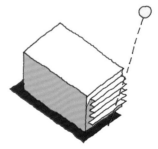

5. Other shading device to deal with high angle sun

30. SUMMER SHADING – SOLUTIONS FOR EAST- AND WEST-FACING FAÇADES

The problem is different for east- and west-facing openings. The sun is low in the sky, but it still might be strong. Some solutions are:

1. vertical fins
2. vertical 'garden'

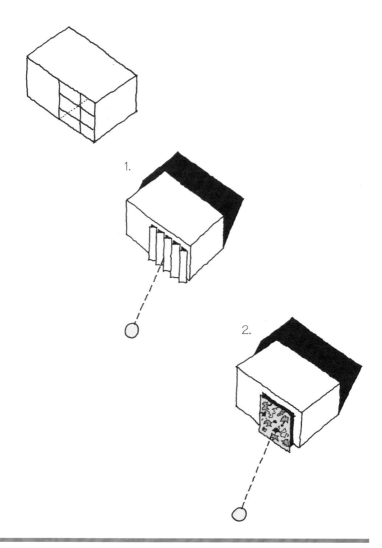

1.

2.

31. SPRING AND AUTUMN – TO SHADE OR NOT TO SHADE?

Solar geometry dictates that the angle of the sun at the spring equinox is the same as that in the autumn. However, in early spring in temperate climates we might want to take advantage of free solar heating, while in autumn we may wish to exclude the still-powerful sun. Inventive shading solutions are needed. Two ideas are indicated right.

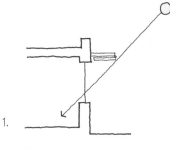

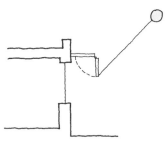

1.

Spring   Autumn

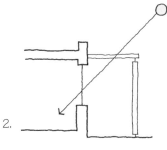

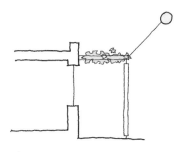

2.

Spring   Autumn

32. CAPTURE THE SUN'S FREE SOURCE OF HEAT

Passive solar design – that is, design that seeks to reduce its reliance on active systems (which require energy inputs) for heating and cooling – takes advantage of the sun. Often, the sun's energy is captured with the aid of 'thermal mass', the capacity for heavy materials to store heat.

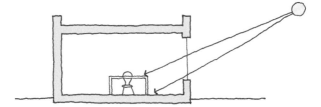

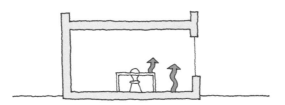

33. COMPACT BUILDINGS USE LESS ENERGY

The greater the surface area of a building envelope, the more energy will be needed to overcome heat losses. A sphere has the smallest surface area by volume of any form. In regions where winter heating is needed, a sprawling single-storey building might use 25% more energy than a compact two-storey cube of the same floor area because it has a greater surface area through which heat is lost. A slightly elongated solar-oriented form provides the best balance between heat loss and beneficial solar gain.

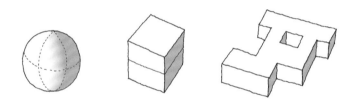

More energy used

34. ORIENTATION, ORIENTATION, ORIENTATION

Knowing the orientation of a building in relation to the sun and wind is fundamental to climate-responsive architecture. Orientation dictates whether solar shading is needed (hot or temperate climates) or winter sun is desirable (cool or temperate regions) and whether a windbreak will be effective. Always put a north arrow on your drawings, and carry a compass at all times in order to check your global position and orientation.

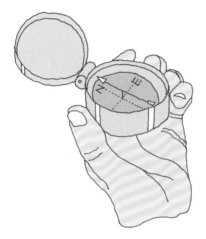

CHAPTER 3
THE LOW ENERGY BUILDING ENVELOPE

- •Heavy and lightweight construction
- •The timing of heating needs
- •Reducing heat loss

35. THINK 'FREE RUNNING'

The diagrams illustrate the designer's job: to use the four-stage design process to squeeze the outdoor climate – the thick black line – into the indoor comfort zone – the green box. Imagine a 'free running' building, one totally unplugged and without any energy inputs: it will gradually settle into a direct response to the external conditions. A well-designed building will provide conditions close to the indoor comfort zone for most or all of the year even when it is free running. Imagine your building design free running – how well will it perform?

In stage 4, there is a choice for occupants: to use energy or to adapt to the environment by changing their behaviour, such as activity or type of clothing. The aim is to minimise the energy needed by succeeding in the first three stages.

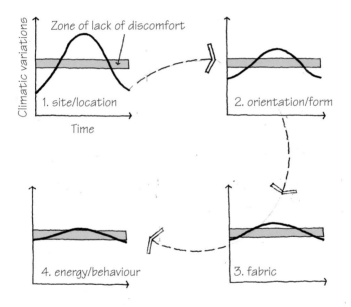

36. HEAVY BUILDINGS HEAT UP AND COOL DOWN SLOWLY

Heavy walls, which have a high thermal mass, will absorb heat slowly and store it. The stored heat will then be released slowly into the building. In high-thermal-mass buildings, the highest indoor temperature will occur in the early hours of the morning, many hours after the highest outdoor temperature has been reached. Heavy buildings are therefore said to have a slow response time. This is also known as the 'thermal flywheel effect', and it relates to the patterns of use of buildings.

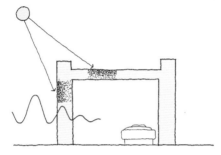

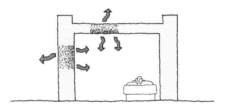

37. LIGHTWEIGHT BUILDINGS HEAT UP AND COOL DOWN QUICKLY

Unlike heavy buildings, a light building will heat up and cool down only slightly more slowly than the conditions outdoors. Lightweight buildings are therefore said to have a quick response time.

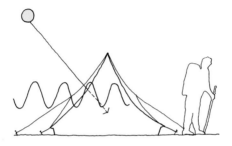

38. THERMAL MASS KEEPS TEMPERATURES STEADY

In temperate climates the main use of thermal mass is to dampen diurnal temperature changes, resulting in a stable internal thermal environment. It does this by absorbing heat gained – directly or indirectly – from the sun and from internal sources such as occupants and equipment, and releasing it slowly during the cooler overnight period. With thermal mass slowing the passage of heat, a time lag of, say, 12 hours might be experienced between the maximum outdoor and maximum indoor temperature. The highest internal temperature can therefore be designed to occur while a building is unoccupied, or where nocturnal ventilation can be employed.

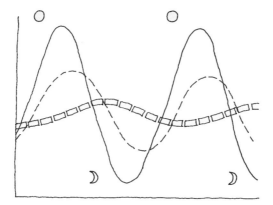

——— Outdoor temperature

— — — Lightweight timber frame building

▭▭▭ Heavyweight building with insulation

39. HIGH THERMAL MASS NEEDS NIGHT-TIME VENTILATION

Thermal mass cannot stop itself from releasing heat. After a day of absorbing heat, from the sun and from internal sources such as people and equipment, it is necessary to flush it away with cooler night-time air. Nocturnal ventilation requires openings, and these need to be designed with security and weather in mind.

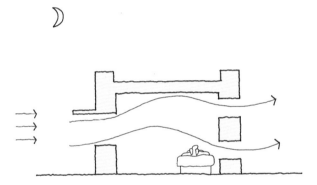

40. THERMAL MASS IS THE OPPOSITE OF INSULATION

Insulation and thermal mass perform different functions. Insulation materials do not store heat well and they resist its flow – they have a high thermal resistance. The reverse is true for thermal mass, which can store heat (or 'coolth') effectively and which has a low resistance to its flow.

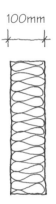

100mm

INSULATION

30 times the insulation
value of brick

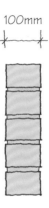

100mm

BRICK

300 times the thermal
storage capacity of
insulation

41. THERMAL MASS AND INSULATION WORK TOGETHER

A heavyweight construction can have exactly the same insulation value (or U-value) as a lightweight construction, but the heavy construction will have many times the thermal mass. A useful rule of thumb is that 25mm of insulation has about the same insulation value as a 1m thickness of concrete. Thermal mass will store heat, and a well-insulated envelope will minimise heat loss. The combination leads to good year-round internal comfort conditions, as long as solar control and nocturnal ventilation are adopted.

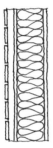

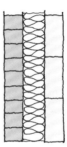

a. Light weight timber frame   b. Heavy weight masonry

a. and b. may have the same insulation value
but b. will have many times the thermal mass

42. ALL MATERIALS HAVE INSULATION AND THERMAL-STORAGE PROPERTIES

The relative insulation and thermal-storage values of different materials help us to decide which construction methods to use in different climatic conditions and for different building functions. It is instructive, for example, to note that a rammed-earth construction has a relatively low insulation value but a very large capacity to store heat: adding insulation would bring the benefits of both properties.

Relative insulation value

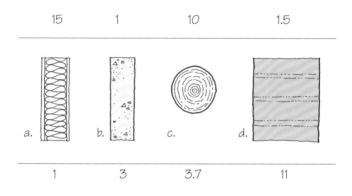

15	1	10	1.5
a.	b.	c.	d.
1	3	3.7	11

Relative thermal storage capacity

a. 150mm timber stud wall
b. 150mm concrete
c. 300mm diameter turned log
d. 450mm rammed earth

43. PUT THERMAL MASS IN ITS RIGHT PLACE

The storage and temperature steadying properties of thermal mass should be used in climates where there is a diurnal temperature difference of more than 6°C (10.8°F), or in cool or cold climates. Thermal mass needs to be exposed both to the sun and to internal heat gains from people and equipment. Internally, for maximum effectiveness the exposed area of a high-thermal-mass floor should be around six times the area of the window that exposes it to the sun.

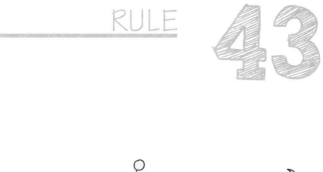

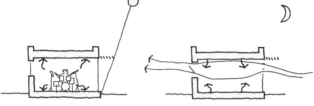

Summer

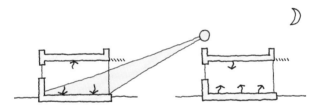

Winter

44. HEAVY OR LIGHTWEIGHT – IT DEPENDS ON CLIMATE

Whether to use high thermal mass or lightweight construction depends on the climate zone and on the building's functions. In hot, arid locations, thermal mass is needed in walls and roof to balance large diurnal temperature differences. In cool and temperate zones, thermal mass is particularly useful in west-facing walls, which are subject to the greatest exposure to solar radiation. For longer, cooler winters (and longer, hotter summers) and in cold climates, internal thermal mass is also beneficial. In hot-humid locations, lightweight construction is preferable. Other than in hot-humid locations, a combination of heavy and light construction will usually be adopted.

CLIMATE ZONE	THERMAL MASS	INSULATION

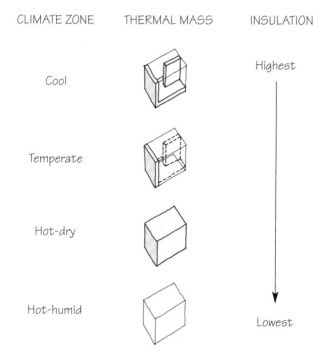

Cool — Highest

Temperate

Hot-dry

Hot-humid — Lowest

45. LIGHTWEIGHT SUITS INTERMITTENT OCCUPATION

A building with intermittent use, which needs to be heated quickly and/or is less sensitive to thermal-comfort requirements, will be more suited to lightweight, quick-response, well-insulated construction. Examples are:

- A home that is occupied only intermittently
- A sports hall
- A market hall

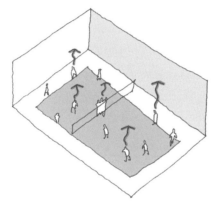

Quick response fabric for intermittent occupation

46. HEAVYWEIGHT SUITS CONTINUOUS OCCUPATION

A building in constant use is more compatible with a heavyweight construction, as temperature swings are dampened and heat is retained for use. Examples are:

- A home occupied all day or used as a home office
- University buildings with 24-hour access
- A hospital

Remember that in an occupied building such as a home, the time lag between maximum outdoor and indoor temperatures could be problematic in warm seasons and regions unless heat is flushed away with cooling nocturnal ventilation.

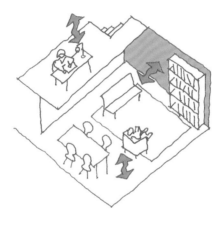

Slow response fabric for continuous occupation

47. COMFORT DEPENDS ON WHAT YOU'RE WEARING AND WHAT YOU'RE DOING

We expect our buildings to provide conditions in which we do not feel uncomfortably hot or cold. Thermal comfort varies from person to person. Our buildings should maintain indoor temperatures of 18–25°C (64.4–77°F) in winter and 20–27°C (68–80.6°F) in summer. People will then alter their clothing and behaviour to find their comfort zone.

48. GLASS – HANDLE WITH CARE

A well-insulated wall will have six times the insulation value of a high-quality double-glazed window, so windows are a very weak link in the building fabric. Glass and windows can be specified to keep heat inside or keep it out, to allow solar heat gain or to block the sun. Many variables exist. The designer's decisions will be influenced by climate, and the diagrams in Chapter 5 consider glass in each climate region of the world.

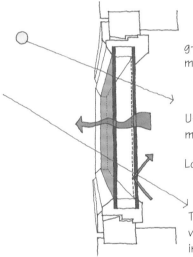

g-value: a high value means more heat gain

U-value: a low value means more insulation

Low-E coating keeps heat in

Transmission of visible light varies: tinted glass allows in little daylight

49. FABRIC FIRST

Buildings lose and gain heat through their fabric – the walls, roof and floor. Insulation is a barrier to heat flows, both in and out of a building, and is needed to maintain thermal comfort. The basic rule is to wrap the building continuously on all sides, including the ground-floor slab, with insulation, which will need to be 200–300mm thick in cold and temperate climates. Heat losses and gains also occur due to infiltration of air from outside to inside, mostly through construction junctions that are not airtight. For retrofit projects, improve the fabric first (adding 75–100mm of insulation is the most cost-effective measure in temperate regions); only then consider renewable energy sources.

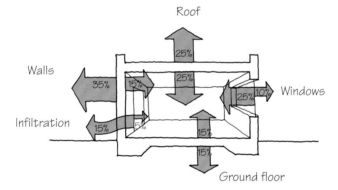

Roof

Walls

Windows

Infiltration

Ground floor

Where heat is typically lost and gained (temperate climate)

50. AN EARTH SHELTER WILL PROVIDE A STABLE THERMAL ENVIRONMENT

Earth sheltering takes advantage of stable temperatures deep in the soil and usually involves burying the building in the ground. The aim is to reduce heat loss and cooling loads. This will result in:

• a warmer indoor environment in winter
• a cooler indoor environment in summer

Ventilation (including nocturnal ventilation) and daylight are important considerations in earth-shelter design, and in most climate regions it is essential to insulate the structure to halt the migration of heat from the building into the surrounding earth. Earth sheltering is considered an expensive construction method and is likely to be adopted mainly on sloping sites and in arid, cool and temperate climate regions.

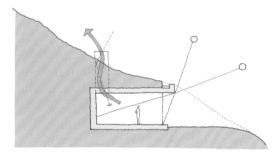

51. A GREEN ROOF PROTECTS AGAINST HEAT LOSS

A thick green roof (500mm or more) will have a high thermal mass, so it will slow the passage of heat by 12 hours or more. It will also need to be insulated, so it will aid significantly in reducing heat loss through the roof. Thin green roofs (150mm of soil) will support only limited planting and 1m deep soil will be needed for small trees.

RULE

Insulation and
water proofing
are needed

200mm for lawn,
1000mm for
small trees

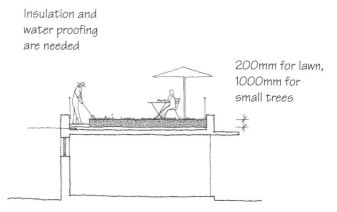

52. INSULATED INTERNAL SHUTTERS KEEP WARMTH IN AT NIGHT

Insulated internal shutters will reduce energy use if drawn across windows to prevent night-time heat loss. On a double-glazed window, they can effectively provide the performance of triple glazing or low-emissivity double glazing. On single glazing, they can upgrade the window's performance to that of double glazing.

○   ☽

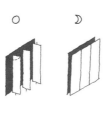

Vertical pivoted

Folding

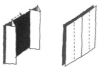

Horizontal pivoted

Sliding

CHAPTER 4
ENERGY AND THE INTERNAL ENVIRONMENT

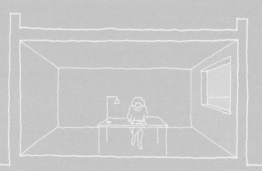

- Free heating: direct, isolated and indirect solar gain
- Free cooling: using earth, wind and water
- Free lighting: daylight
- Colour

53. WE ARE AN INDOOR SPECIES

As a rule of thumb, in the so-called developed regions of the world we spend about 90% of our time inside buildings. We use mainly fossil-fuel-derived energy to maintain comfort conditions within those buildings, and the production of that energy results in the release of CO_2, a greenhouse gas linked with global warming and climate change. Unless we revert to being a mainly outdoor species, we must reduce our energy use.

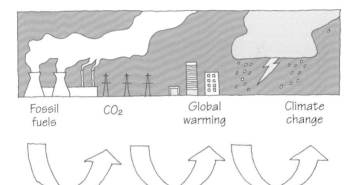

| Fossil fuels | CO_2 | Global warming | Climate change |

54. COMBINE DIRECT SOLAR GAIN WITH THERMAL MASS

Using occupied spaces as the passive heating system of a building is an effective strategy, especially in combination with thermal mass. The sun must be permitted to enter the building during the heating season – a window facing within 30° of south (north in the southern hemisphere) will do – and when combined with internal heat gains such as those from people and equipment, and with a heat-recovery system, a building may be passively heated for much or all of the winter. Climate-responsive buildings in cool climates therefore aim to take advantage of solar-oriented windows for direct solar gain, and minimise openings in the opposite façade.

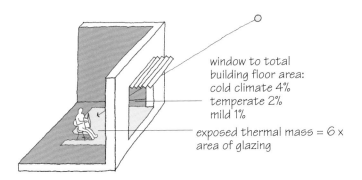

window to total
building floor area:
cold climate 4%
temperate 2%
mild 1%

exposed thermal mass = 6 x
area of glazing

55. CAPTURE FREE HEAT WITH A SUNSPACE

Heat captured by a glazed solar-oriented (or within 45° of south/north) sunspace can be redistributed into occupied spaces. The sunspace is usually coupled convectively, meaning that the heat is transferred by opening doors or windows in an insulated wall between sunspace and building. This is known as 'isolated solar gain'. A sunspace may be an occupied space but it will be subject to large temperature swings, like a greenhouse, unless carefully designed with high-performance glass and summer shading. Make the area of solar-oriented glazing about 10% of the floor area of the building to be heated, and combine the heat source with natural ventilation to distribute heat.

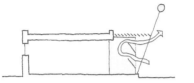

summer

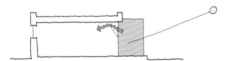

winter

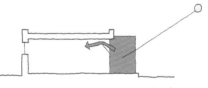

spring/autumn

56. WARM AIR WANTS TO BE COOL

Warm air molecules contain more energy than those in cool air. Any mass of warm air will try to attain equilibrium by moving towards colder air. Thus, if outside air is warmer than the air inside a building it can be a heat source, flowing into the cooler building. Conversely, if outdoor air is cooler than that inside, such as at night, it will act as a heat sink, drawing warm air outwards. The same thermal dynamics occur within a building as warm air always moves to occupy cooler spaces, so buildings should be planned to keep heated air in the spaces where it is needed or to encourage it to move there.

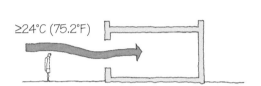

≥24°C (75.2°F)

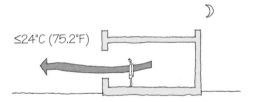

≤24°C (75.2°F)

57. A TROMBE WALL FREELY TRANSMITS HEAT TO INSIDE

A Trombe wall is an indirect-solar-gain assembly constructed of a high-mass material such as masonry or concrete. The solar-oriented wall of 300–400mm thickness sits behind a glazed façade, which reduces heat loss, and it is usually painted black to aid heat absorption. Top and bottom vents in the wall mean that in addition to thermal conduction it takes advantage of convection in order to transfer heat to occupied spaces. The Trombe wall area should be about 10% of the floor area of the building to be heated.

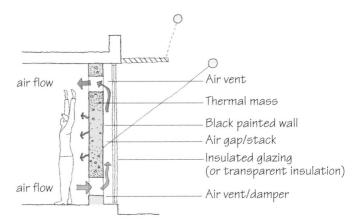

air flow

air flow

Air vent

Thermal mass

Black painted wall

Air gap/stack

Insulated glazing
(or transparent insulation)

Air vent/damper

58. WATER CAN STORE MORE HEAT THAN CONCRETE

Water, in fact, has the capacity to store about four times as much heat as concrete. A water wall is similar to a Trombe wall, but in this case mass is replaced with water, which may be stored in a range of containers (pipes, steel tanks or drums, fibreglass vessels) and which heats up and cools slowly. When associated with natural ventilation, the water wall may also be used for free cooling. Its area should be about 10% of the floor area of the building to be heated. The water wall should contain around 200 litres of water per square metre of glazing; tanks should be approximately 450mm deep.

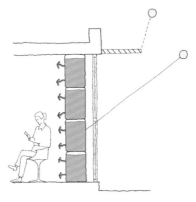

59. A POND ON THE ROOF IS A FREE SOURCE OF HEAT

Working in a similar way to the water wall, a pond roof is an indirect-solar-gain device that collects heat from the sun and slowly releases it by conduction through the roof to the occupied spaces below. In temperate climate zones, the pond will be insulated during the night to reduce heat loss. Spaces below the pond roof may be 3–4°C (5.4–7.2°F) warmer than they would be without the thermal storage pond.

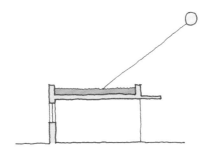

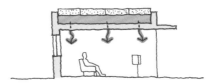

60. HARVEST THE SUN'S HEAT FROM THE EARTH

The relative warmth below the surface of the earth in cool and temperate climates can be exploited by enabling an exchange of this heat into coils of fluid-filled pipes. The coils (often referred to as 'slinky' coils) are connected to a ground source heat pump. This enables the earth's stored heat, the source of which is the sun, to be transferred from the buried coils, via the heat pump, into a building – often using an underfloor heating system. The earth will act as a heat source in winter and a heat sink in the summer. For a typical house, a designer's rule of thumb would be to use three 10m long trenches with slinky coils (totalling 200m of pipe) of 25mm diameter pipe buried 1.8m deep. The heat pump can be powered by the sun.

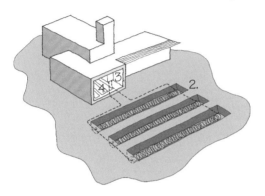

1. sun warms earth

2. refrigerant in coils collects earth-stored heat

3. ground source heat pump up-grades to useful temperature

4. underfloor heating supplied by heat pump

61. RECOVER AND REUSE VALUABLE HEAT

In a heating season (a winter in temperate and cool climates), heat generated in spaces such as kitchens and bathrooms can be recovered rather than expelled, and the heat exchanged with incoming fresh air, which, now warmed, is recirculated to where it is needed. Such systems need a well insulated and airtight envelope. At its most extreme, or in large complex buildings where the rules of thumb for natural ventilation might not be applicable, the whole building might adopt year-round mechanical ventilation with heat recovery (MVHR) as long as it is airtight and super-insulated.

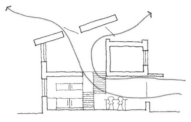

summer

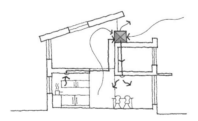

winter

62. STORE SUMMER HEAT FOR USE IN THE WINTER

The idea of an inter-seasonal store is to harvest and store heat in the summer months for use in the winter, or coolth in winter for summer use. For heating, a storage medium such as water is heated in a highly insulated vessel using solar energy. A temperature of between 30 and 40°C (86 and 104°F) is suitable for running an underfloor heating system, unlike a traditional heating system that needs 60 to 90°C (140 to 194°F), and this can be provided by an inter-seasonal solar-energy store. Alternative seasonal storage methods range from using the earth itself to rock or borehole water deep under its surface, and to employing phase-change materials.

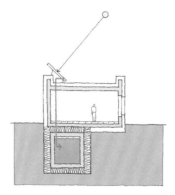

summer

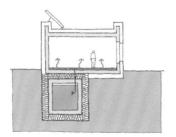

winter

63. HARNESS THE WIND TO PROVIDE NATURAL VENTILATION

We ventilate buildings in order to provide thermal comfort and oxygen, and to dispel odours. Two of the natural forces relating to air, wind and buoyancy, are used to naturally ventilate buildings. Wind meeting a building creates a pressure difference between its windward and leeward faces, and this drives ventilation.

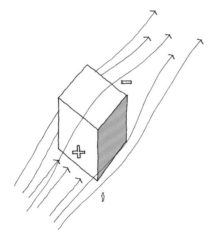

64. WARM AIR RISES, DRAWING COOLER AIR IN

The basic principle is that hot air rises due to buoyancy. The temperature difference between warm air inside and cooler air outside a building causes the air inside to rise, drawing cool, fresh air in at the lower levels and expelling warm, stale air higher up.

65. A RULE OF THUMB FOR SINGLE-SIDED VENTILATION

For spaces that have access to the outside on only one face, single-sided ventilation will work up to a maximum room depth of 6m. An openable window is normally used because it can provide both ventilation and daylight. Allow an opening area of at least 5% of the floor area to be ventilated, and considerably more in hot climates or places with low wind speeds.

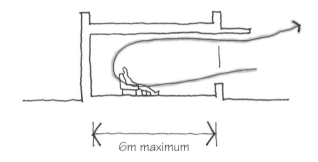

6m maximum

66. A RULE OF THUMB FOR CROSS VENTILATION

Cross ventilation relies on the pressure difference between the windward and leeward faces of a building. It will work as long as the depth of the space is no more than five times its height. There must be wind for cross ventilation to work, and both the inlet and outlet openings should be at least 5% of the floor area.

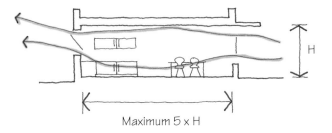

Maximum 5 x H

67. A RULE OF THUMB FOR STACK VENTILATION

Stack ventilation, which relies on buoyancy of air, works whenever there is a temperature difference of more than about 2°C (3.6°F) between outside and inside.

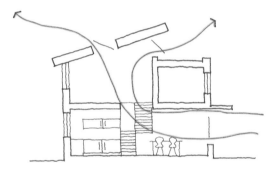

68. IN A HOT CLIMATE, KEEP THE EARTH AROUND A BUILDING COOL

Shaded or water-cooled earth beneath and around a building can act as a source of free cooling, particularly in arid or hot-humid locations, because earth that is protected from solar radiation will be cooler than the outdoor air temperature. The use of earth cooling pipes (see Rule 70) enables the cooled earth to transfer coolth to ventilation air. Alternatively, by raising a building off the ground in hot-humid locations the earth beneath is cooled by summer rains and evaporation, providing another means of cooling the ventilation air.

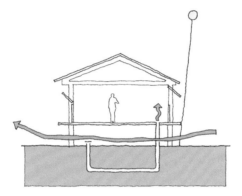

69. WITH SHADING, A POND ON THE ROOF WILL KEEP THE BUILDING COOL

Just as it is a good medium for storing heat, water will also act as a store of coolth. As a roof pond, it needs to be shallow (around 150–300mm deep) and must be shaded during the daytime to prevent solar heat gain – shaded water will be much cooler than exposed water. With such a pool located above an occupied space, evaporative cooling is achieved with no increase in indoor humidity. A pond roof has been found to modify the outdoor maximum temperature by up to 13°C (23.4°F). Technical problems to be overcome with inventive design include the weight of water and the need for shade and insulation above the water.

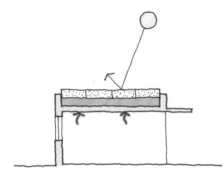

70. PIPE IN AIR THAT HAS BEEN COOLED BY THE EARTH

Used mainly to assist in cooling in hot-arid climates, earth cooling pipes take advantage of stable temperatures under the surface of the earth. Air inside the buried pipes is cooled by the earth temperature. The soil temperature must be considerably lower than the desirable room-air temperature, and the system is best for buildings with higher-than-normal ventilation rates (eg schools). The pipes need to be buried at least 1.8m deep; they should be 150–300mm in diameter, and about 40m in total length. A fan is used to move air through the earth pipes.

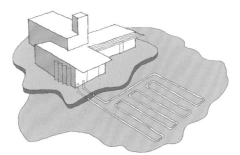

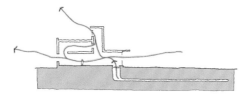

Section showing ventilation with heating/cooling
aided by earth pipes

71. USE DAYLIGHT TO REDUCE ENERGY USE

Daylight is a free, plentiful and reliable natural resource. We need about 100 lux for occasional reading and 300 lux for continuous tasks. Many times this quantity of daylight exists outside, even on overcast days: in direct sunlight, we experience 100,000 lux. And yet, we rely too often on energy-hungry artificial lighting in our buildings. Up to 50% of the energy used in a typical office building is used for artificial lighting, and this figure is 90% for shops and over 20% for schools. A by-product of much artificial lighting is heat, which is not always a desirable property – particularly in warm seasons or hotter climate zones. So we should aim to efficiently capture daylight and put it to use where it is needed. A daylighting strategy might save up to 40% of energy consumption over an artificial lighting scheme.

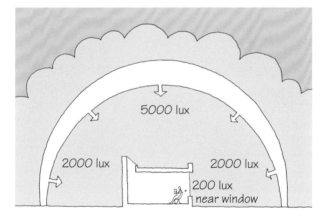

5000 lux

2000 lux

2000 lux

200 lux
near window

72. HOW MUCH SKY CAN THE BUILDING 'SEE'?

The amount of daylight entering a building is a function of how much sky the building can 'see' and so the size and position of windows are crucial design matters. Daylight and views are compromised below the No Sky Line and a room will appear gloomy if more than 50% of the working plane is beyond the line.

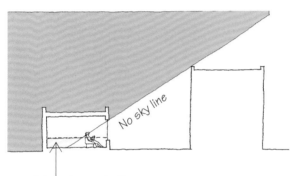

No sky line

Below the no sky line

73. FOR THE RIGHT AMOUNT OF DAYLIGHT YOU NEED THE RIGHT SIZE OF WINDOW

In a small-to-medium-sized space with windows to one side, the window needs to comprise around 20% of the wall area. This applies to rooms of up to about 7m in depth. For deeper spaces, the required window area increases to 35%. Large-volume spaces will generally be most efficiently lit with rooflights.

Window = 20% of wall

74. A TALL WINDOW THROWS DAYLIGHT DEEP INTO A ROOM

Sidelighting – where a room has windows to one side only – can provide effective lighting for plan depths up to twice the height of the window. Tall windows in higher rooms result in a greater throw of light deeper into the room, and greater uniformity in the distribution of daylight. Energy-efficient buildings are usually not deep in plan, but have maximum overall plan depths of 12–14 m, which, incidentally, is the maximum rule-of-thumb depth for both daylight and natural ventilation.

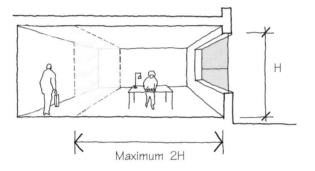

Maximum 2H

H

75. DAYLIGHT IS MORE PLENTIFUL OVERHEAD

Assuming the same area of glazing as a window in a wall in Rule 73, toplighting will provide 2.5 times as much daylight. Rooflights are therefore very effective, but they must be protected from solar gain. They are also a potentially significant cause of heat loss in cool and temperate climates. The area of a rooflight will need to be approximately 10–15% of the floor area to be daylit.

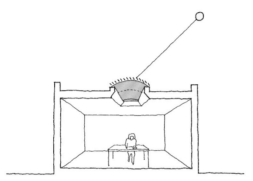

76. USE ROOFLIGHTS TO BRING DAYLIGHT INTO LARGE SPACES

There is a relationship between the height of a space and the number and separation of rooflights. Larger spaces may be lit with monitors, skylights or a sawtooth (or 'northlight') form.

½H H H ½H

H

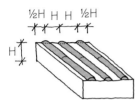

Rooflights

2½H   4H   2½H

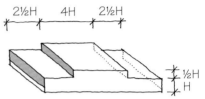

½H
H

Monitor

2H   H   2H

H

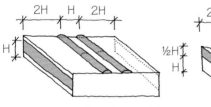

Rooflights with
side lighting

2½H 2½H 2½H

½H
H

Sawtooth
(or northlighting)

77. LIGHT INTERIORS NEED SMALLER WINDOWS

The window-facing back wall of a room, in particular, must have a high reflectance value, which may be achieved by using white paint. The further the window is from a room's rear wall, the higher the reflectance of the finishes will need to be if artificial lighting is to be avoided. Reflectance of daylight from a light shelf and from light-coloured external ground finishes (eg white or light stone, snow) throws natural light deeper into a space, further improving daylight distribution. A room with dark interior finishes will need almost twice the window area of a light-coloured reflective room, and this increases heat loss and/or heat gain.

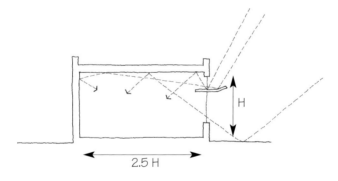

78. EXTERIOR COLOUR INFLUENCES ENERGY USE

A black wall or roof will absorb up to 20 times the solar energy of one which is white. In climates with cool/cold winters, darker, absorptive solar-oriented roofs and façades will provide beneficial heat gains. However, in summer a heat-reflecting surface is desirable in warm/hot climates and seasons. In hot desert regions, where solar intensity is high, and aside from the problem of glare, white buildings will always be favoured. The roof of a building receives more solar radiation in summer than any other surface, regardless of latitude, and a white roof will typically remain at lower-than-air temperature.

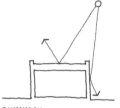

summer

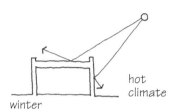

winter

hot
climate

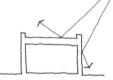

summer

winter

temperate
climate

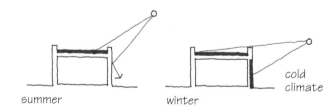

summer   winter

cold
climate

79. KEEP IT SIMPLE

Building occupants will ignore or override complex controls and systems. Over time, they will forget how a building works. However, people feel more comfortable when they have some control of their environment, so low energy-use architecture needs to be robust, intuitive and simple.

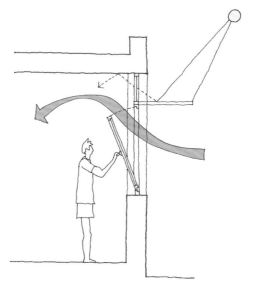

80. GIVE CLEAR INSTRUCTIONS

Users of buildings need to know how the building works. In order that occupants do not forget how to manage their environment over time, provide an operating manual that explains how the building works, day and night, throughout ithe seasons.

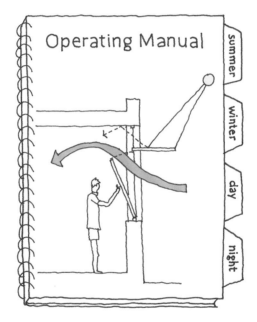

Operating Manual

summer

winter

day

night

CHAPTER 5
RULES AND STRATEGIES FOR DIFFERENT CLIMATIC REGIONS

- Hot-dry climate
- Hot-humid climate
- Cold climate
- Cold-winter/hot-summer climate
- Temperate climate

81. DESIGN FOR YOUR CLIMATE

The basic rule is that in cold climates we should aim to keep heat in (with insulation) and in hot climates we need to keep the sun out (with shading and light colours). In the following pages, the rules of thumb for different climatic regions are illustrated with the use of some imagined buildings. The different construction methods, planning factors (location of rooms, etc.), form, orientation and natural heating/cooling techniques are shown.

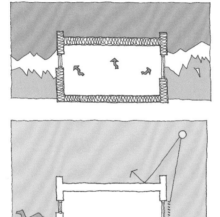

4 RULES FOR:

HOT-DRY CLIMATE

82. The key is to slow the rate of indoor heating on summer days using thermal mass and shading.

83. Promote rapid cooling on summer evenings with wind towers and/or cross ventilation.

84. Use natural cooling in summer, with water if available.

85. Use natural heating in winter, so orientation and opening design for solar gain are crucial.

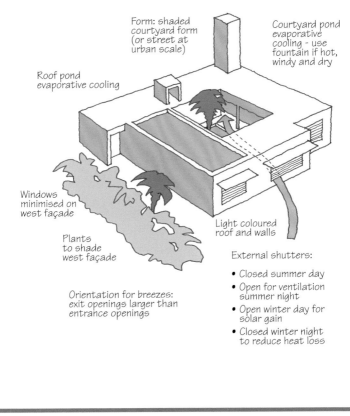

Form: shaded courtyard form (or street at urban scale)

Courtyard pond evaporative cooling - use fountain if hot, windy and dry

Roof pond evaporative cooling

Windows minimised on west façade

Plants to shade west façade

Light coloured roof and walls

External shutters:

- Closed summer day
- Open for ventilation summer night
- Open winter day for solar gain
- Closed winter night to reduce heat loss

Orientation for breezes: exit openings larger than entrance openings

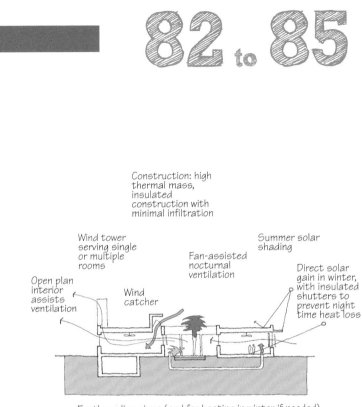

Construction: high thermal mass, insulated construction with minimal infiltration

Wind tower serving single or multiple rooms

Fan-assisted nocturnal ventilation

Summer solar shading

Open plan interior assists ventilation

Wind catcher

Direct solar gain in winter, with insulated shutters to prevent night time heat loss

Earth cooling pipes (and for heating in winter if needed). Basement also takes advantage of earth cooling

Glass and window properties:

• Very low g-value
• Low-E (surface 2)
• Low U-value.
• Shading essential

HOT-HUMID CLIMATE

86. The priority is ventilation: it must be effective, night and day.

87. Reduce solar heating of the building fabric with shading.

88. Permit a high rate of evening cooling with large openings and cross ventilation.

89. Allow natural cooling using shaded ground, evaporative cooling and wind.

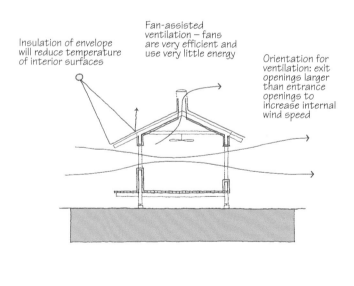

Construction: lightweight construction generally preferable although thermal mass will provide temperature stability with night purging

Insulation of envelope will reduce temperature of interior surfaces

Fan-assisted ventilation – fans are very efficient and use very little energy

Orientation for ventilation: exit openings larger than entrance openings to increase internal wind speed

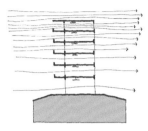

Tall buildings can take advantage of the higher wind speeds higher above the earth's surface

High-level ventilation such as wind-driven, could be linked with double skin roof construction

Glass and window properties:
• Very low g-value,
• Low-E (surface 2),
• Low U-value.
• Shading essential

Light colours to reflect solar radiation, reducing fabric heat gains

Form: narrow plan form assists cross ventilation. Alternative is open plan with large envelope area to increase rate of cooling

Orientation for wind direction and maximum solar shading

Large openings to maximize ventilation

Solar shading: balconies, porches, brise soleil and roof overhangs for solar control

Building on stilts for cooled earth and ventilation cooling of floor (also to protect against flooding)

Avoid windbreaks to maximise ventilation around buildings

COLD CLIMATE

90. The goal is reduced heating-energy needs using buffer zones, insulation and minimal infiltration.

91. Permit natural heating using solar gain.

92. Allow summer ventilation.

93. Super-insulation with thermal mass requires good ventilation in order to prevent overheating.

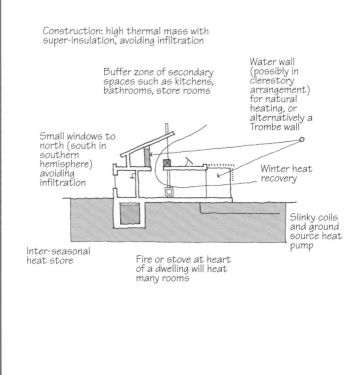

Construction: high thermal mass with super-insulation, avoiding infiltration

Buffer zone of secondary spaces such as kitchens, bathrooms, store rooms

Water wall (possibly in clerestory arrangement) for natural heating, or alternatively a Trombe wall

Small windows to north (south in southern hemisphere) avoiding infiltration

Winter heat recovery

Slinky coils and ground source heat pump

Inter-seasonal heat store

Fire or stove at heart of a dwelling will heat many rooms

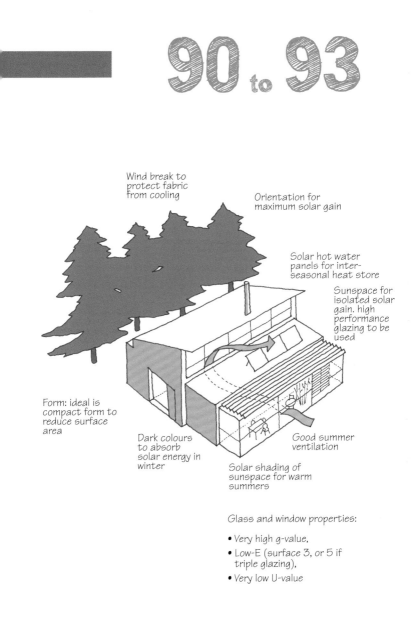

Wind break to protect fabric from cooling

Orientation for maximum solar gain

Solar hot water panels for inter-seasonal heat store

Sunspace for isolated solar gain. high performance glazing to be used

Form: ideal is compact form to reduce surface area

Dark colours to absorb solar energy in winter

Good summer ventilation

Solar shading of sunspace for warm summers

Glass and window properties:

• Very high g-value,
• Low-E (surface 3, or 5 if triple glazing),
• Very low U-value

4 RULES FOR:

COLD-WINTER/HOT-SUMMER CLIMATE

94. The goal is reduced heating-energy needs using buffer zones and insulation, together with reduced infiltration.

95. Use natural heating and cooling with sun and wind.

96. Allow good summer ventilation, including nocturnal ventilation.

97. Do not block summer breezes with a winter windbreak.

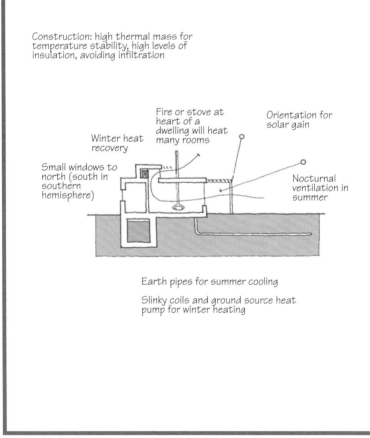

Construction: high thermal mass for temperature stability, high levels of insulation, avoiding infiltration

Fire or stove at heart of a dwelling will heat many rooms

Orientation for solar gain

Winter heat recovery

Small windows to north (south in southern hemisphere)

Nocturnal ventilation in summer

Earth pipes for summer cooling

Slinky coils and ground source heat pump for winter heating

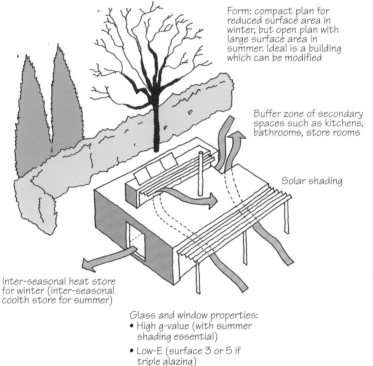

Landscape: summer shading of ground, winter wind break

Form: compact plan for reduced surface area in winter, but open plan with large surface area in summer. Ideal is a building which can be modified

Buffer zone of secondary spaces such as kitchens, bathrooms, store rooms

Solar shading

Inter-seasonal heat store for winter (inter-seasonal coolth store for summer)

Glass and window properties:
• High g-value (with summer shading essential)
• Low-E (surface 3 or 5 if triple glazing)
• Very low U-value

4 RULES FOR:

TEMPERATE CLIMATE

98. The goal is reduced heating-energy needs using buffer zones and insulation to reduce winter heat loss.

99. Prevent overheating in summer with thermal mass (and nocturnal ventilation) for temperature stability, shading as needed.

100. Use natural heating in winter.

101. Reduced air infiltration is a must: sheltered entrances and wind lobbies included.

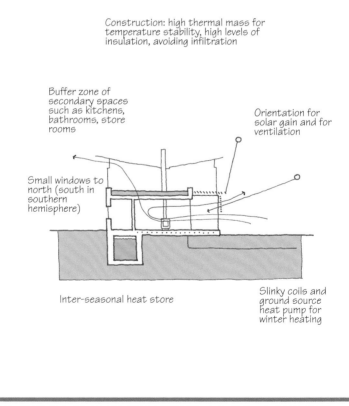

Construction: high thermal mass for temperature stability, high levels of insulation, avoiding infiltration

Buffer zone of secondary spaces such as kitchens, bathrooms, store rooms

Orientation for solar gain and for ventilation

Small windows to north (south in southern hemisphere)

Inter-seasonal heat store

Slinky coils and ground source heat pump for winter heating

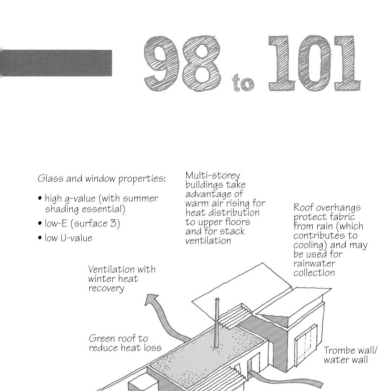

Glass and window properties:

- high g-value (with summer shading essential)
- low-E (surface 3)
- low U-value

Multi-storey buildings take advantage of warm air rising for heat distribution to upper floors and for stack ventilation

Roof overhangs protect fabric from rain (which contributes to cooling) and may be used for rainwater collection

Ventilation with winter heat recovery

Green roof to reduce heat loss

Trombe wall/ water wall

Warm rooms to solar-oriented face (cold rooms as buffer opposite)

Sheltered entrance with wind lobby

Sunspace coupled with interior spaces. Solar shading to prevent overheating in summer

Sheltering walls and planting as wind buffer

Notes, observations and references – a narrative bibliography

The rules of thumb result from more than 30 years of learning and teaching, architectural practice, research, travel, observation, reading, talking, listening and thinking. Not every rule of thumb has a body of literature or academic enquiry behind it, or an equation to define it. Many do, however, and the following notes are intended to be helpful to the reader who wishes to know some more of the background to the rules, or where to find out more information. The notes make reference to books and online resources that have inspired this author, and the references are linked to the bibliography.

A NOTE ON THERMAL COMFORT

There is much research and a great deal has been written on the subject of thermal comfort and various models exist for defining it. The problem is that many factors influence the feeling of human comfort, including temperature, humidity, indoor air speed, clothing, body shape, gender, activity etc. In brief, so-called static models assume that there should be an unchanging indoor temperature regardless of season or location, whereas adaptive models take account of varying external conditions and the possibility that occupants will actively adapt to their internal environment.

Much of what is written is purely technical or scientific research into the performance of buildings, and so is difficult for the non-scientist to fully comprehend, but the subject is also about human feelings. It is helpful to refer to Michael Humphrey's illustration of the adaptive approach in 'Thermal Comfort Temperatures and the Habits of Hobbits' (contained within Standards for Thermal Comfort: Indoor Air Temperature Standards for the 21st Century (1995, pp3-43). We are reminded in this paper too that humans found ways to build comfortable environments long before we were able to model and predict their performance, and this is what the rules of thumb are about.

Chappells and Shove in Comfort: A Review of Philosophies and Paradigms (2004) have provided an excellent review of the literature and ideas relating to many aspects of human comfort throughout modern history and the work contains useful references. Comfort is variable and will be interpreted differently by different people in different climatic regions. I remember that my own teachers did not use the term 'comfort zone', they used 'zone of lack of discomfort' because the aim is to explain the conditions in which most people would not feel uncomfortable. Baruch Givoni discusses the physiology which enables humans to adapt to their environment in a book which sits permanently on my desk, Climate Considerations in Building and Urban Design. Here (pp3–36) he sets out his opinion that differing comfort standards should be adopted for different climatic regions.

CHAPTER 1: WORKING WITH SITE AND LOCATION

Buildings and energy

Brian Edwards, in his comprehensive reference volume *The Rough Guide to Sustainability* (2007, p67) discusses the link between fossil fuel combustion and CO_2 emissions and there are some further, useful statistics relating to the energy used in buildings in a paper published by the United States Environmental Protection Agency, titled: Buildings and their Impact on the Environment: A Statistical Summary, (2009, p2). It is of interest to note that households spend on average $2,000 per year on energy bills, and that more than half of this sum goes on providing thermal comfort and satisfactory lighting.

The sun and solar geometry

A basic understanding of solar geometry and the ability to read sun-path diagrams are key skills for the designer of low energy architecture and there is a concise explanation of solar geometry and of the relationship between sun and earth by Bougdah and Sharples in *Environment, Technology and Sustainability*, Volume 2 (2010, pp19–26). Using a sun-path diagram, the sun's position in terms of both altitude (angle above the horizon) and azimuth (position in relation to the compass points) can be determined for any time of day at any place on the planet. Web-based sun-path calculators are readily available and they give an instant and detailed result, including sunrise and sunset times, but they do not give the whole picture in one view, as a sunpath diagram does. A description of sun-path diagrams, and an explanation of how to use them may be found in *Sun, Wind and Light: Architectural Design Strategies* (2001, p8) and a range of northern hemisphere sunpath diagrams are included in Appendix A, (pp323–327) of that volume. Websites such as www.gaisma.com and www.jaloxa.eu provide a complete range of diagrams either by location or by latitude.

Topography and wind

Bougdah and Sharples, in *Environment, Technology and Sustainability*, Volume 2 (2010, pp27–34 and pp41–43) provide helpful diagrams indicating the effects of wind flow in relation to buildings and landscape. They, and Randall Thomas in *Environmental Design, an Introduction for Architects and Engineers* (2006, p63) provide descriptions and diagrams of the effects of windbreaks. The UK Building Research Establishment (BRE), Digest 350, *Climate and Site Development Part 3: Improving Microclimate Through Design* (1990) further interrogates implications and solutions in relation to buildings' sensitivity to wind.

The United States Department of Agriculture (Natural Resources

Conservation Service) has a website which contains a wealth of general and technical information on windbreak design, including appropriate plant species, and suggests that a well-designed windbreak protecting a rural building can result in energy savings in winter heating costs of 15 to 25% because cooling of the building envelope and, importantly, air infiltration are reduced. The strength of the wind matters, and Olgyay, in *Design With Climate* (1963, p99) tells us that the heating requirement for a house subject to a 20mph wind would be 2.4 times that of the same house in a 5mph wind. Where trees are used both as windbreaks and for summer shading overall energy savings of up to 40% have been reported in studies on Farmstead Windbreaks by Quam, Wight and Hirning at North Dakota State University (1993). Their work contains further useful information on windbreak composition and very good explanatory diagrams of windbreak designs. The effects of hilly topography on wind are discussed by Dean Hawkes et al in *The Selective Environment, An Approach to Environmentally Responsive Architecture* (2002, pp124–125 and 128–130) and covered comprehensively, with diagrams, by Brown and DeKay in their essential handbook *Sun, Wind and Light* (2001, pp17–23).

Water and landscape for cooling

The BRE document *Environmental Site Layout Planning: Solar Access, Microclimate and Passive Cooling in Urban Areas* (2000, pp37–43) by Littlefair et al provides references to research which confirms our intuition that bodies of water will provide a source of cooling. The larger the body of water the better is the rule. A lake might provide a reduction in air temperature in its vicinity of up to 2°C (3.6°F). However, a small pool in a garden, if it replaces materials which would otherwise readily absorb and re-radiate heat, will have a much larger local cooling effect.

Trees and cooling

Trees, which absorb radiation and cool the surrounding air, can lower the air temperature near buildings and therefore lower the indoor temperature, although there seems to be little hard evidence and few agreed rules. In *Environmental Site Layout Planning* Littlefair et al (2000, p40) cite evidence suggesting that the temperature will be lowered in this way for a distance of up to five times the height of an orchard, and that the temperature drop within and downwind of a forest might be as much as 6°C (10.8°F).

Green spaces in cities do not merely provide an environment for recreation but bring beneficial cooling for a considerable distance, 150m or more into the urban fabric according to Baruch Givoni in *Climate Considerations in Building and Urban Design* (1998, pp308–310). The urban issues are dealt with in further detail by Brown and DeKay in *Sun, Wind and Light: Architectural Design Strategies* (2001, pp121–124).

Trees and their leaves

The UK Building Research Establishment (BRE) Digest 350, *Climate and Site Development Part 3: Improving Microclimate Through Design* (1990, p6) lists the transparency of different species of tree crowns to solar radiation and the range of their foliation periods. As an example, deciduous trees in the UK will be in full leaf from about May to September and there will be a period of a month or so at each end of this period when they will be in partial leaf, before and after which they will be quite bare. This is the type of information useful to the low energy designer who can manipulate orientation, form and openings to benefit from tree shade or permit access to winter sunlight.

Further strategic design comment, along with foliation data for trees in the United States may be found in *Sun, Wind and Light: Architectural Design Strategies* Brown and DeKay (2001, pp268 and 269), and in other countries and regions similar reference material on the characteristics of local tree species may be consulted and applied to shading and passive solar designs.

The position of a shade-giving tree in relation to a building façade is discussed by Thomas (2006, p59) in *Environmental Design, an Introduction for Architects and Engineers.* Pelsmakers, in *The Environmental Design Pocketbook* (2012, p80), proposes a slightly different rule, which places the trunk of the tree at a distance from the building of 1 to 1.5 times its mature height.

CHAPTER 2. MANIPULATING ORIENTATION AND FORM

Sun and wind

A more complete explanation of global winds may be found in Matthys Levy's (2007) *Why the Wind Blows*, which contains much of interest for the budding meteorologist. *The Rough Guide to Weather* (2007), by Robert Henson provides a good jumping-off point for all things weather-related and gives a concise climatic history of global climatic regions and an explanation of the seasons. The characteristics of each climate region are clearly described by Baruch Givoni in *Climate Considerations in Building and Urban Design* (1998, pp333–441).

Why should the main façade face the sun?

Well, the closer to south (or north in the southern hemisphere) the better is the rule because, as Simos Yannas shows us in *Solar Energy and Housing Design*, Volume 1 (1994, p88), energy use in northern hemisphere housing doubles if windows face mainly east, west or north rather than south.

North-facing windows create a significant energy problem in temperate and cold climates and should be minimised. Randall Thomas, in his very readable environmental science primer *Environmental Design, an Introduction for Architects and Engineers* (2006 p58), confirms the general rule that energy performance will be optimized as long as the main façade – the façade with the greatest solar-oriented window area – is oriented to within 45° of the midday sun. Brown and DeKay, in *Sun, Wind and Light: Architectural Design Strategies* (2001, p167, quoting Balcomb et al: *Passive Solar Design Analysis*, 1984) define the limits more closely, stating that if the façade is within 30° of south the fall-off in solar performance will be less than 10%.

Shading

Well designed solar control shading can almost eliminate solar gain. Pelsmakers (2012, p141), in *The Environmental Design Pocketbook* provides examples of shading devices which would block up to 90% of solar gains. Solar control shading design is determined by the orientation of a building's openings and relates to the time of day and time of the year when a building needs to be shaded. The best way to design solar shading is to model it, either using modelling software or by using physical models and a heliodon, a device which uses a light source to represent the sun's elevation and azimuth at any place and time on the planet. However, for solar-oriented openings the general climate-related rules, which will do as a starting point for design, are:

• Cold and temperate regions: design a horizontal projection for a sun cut-off angle half way between the sun's altitude at midday on the summer and winter solstices, but with a maximum projection of 1.5m. For mid-latitude regions the following formula is sometimes used:

Summer projection = h/tan(ss)

Winter projection = h/tan(ws)

where h = height of window, ss = elevation of sun at summer solstice, ws = elevation of sun at winter solstice. Design the projection to be between the two figures.

• Hot regions: use the altitude of the sun at the spring equinox to determine the depth of the overhang, but bearing in mind that some hot summer regions have cool spring and autumn periods when solar gains are beneficial

• Hot equatorial regions: here the high midday sun can be blocked with a relatively narrow horizontal projection. But the sun may also heat the equator-facing elevation in mid-afternoon for some of the year, and at a much lower angle to the horizon. In these regions the spring equinox at mid afternoon, say 3.00pm, is a better starting point for determining the projection depth. Remember that the sun will also reach the non-equator-facing façade in summer and that a combination of vertical and horizontal projections will usually be the most effective solution for shading of all elevations.

Brown and DeKay, in *Sun, Wind and Light: Architectural Design Strategies* (2001, pp262–267), provide a set of tables which act as a short cut to the formulae and allow some sizing of projections for a range of latitudes and for solar-oriented as well as east and west facing windows. They also describe (pp57–60) a method of determining when shading will be needed, and of what type. There is a wealth of insight and practical guidance in CIBSE *Daylighting and window design: Lighting Guide LG10* (1999) and much is applicable not only to the UK but to other similarly mild, temperate climates.

Spring and autumn equinox issues – to shade or not to shade?

This particular aspect of solar geometry, that the elevation of the sun is the same on both 21 March and 21 September, is often forgotten and the important differences between heating and shading needs at these times must not be missed. The excellent *Passive Solar Architecture Pocket Reference* by Haggard et al (2009, p24) has a good section on shading and covers this issue, as does Pelsmakers in *The Environmental Design Pocketbook* (2012, p141, Fig 6.5.3).

Compact form and ventilation – a dilemma

In some climate regions there is obviously a conflict between the desire for energy-saving compactness on the one hand and a more spread out form which encourages cross ventilation and increases surface area for cooling on the other. Givoni discusses this in *Climate Considerations in Building and Urban Design* (1998, pp50–53) and suggests that an adaptable configuration might be the answer.

Olgyay, in *Design With Climate, Bioclimatic Approach to Architectural Regionalism* (1963, pp87–91) argues that a slightly elongated solar-oriented form provides the best balance between heat loss and beneficial solar gain. The Oikos website's article in Issue 36 has an interesting study of the energy benefits of compact forms, with some helpful numbers. Hall and Nicholls, in *The Green Building Bible* Volume 2 (2006, pp 70–73) present a good explanation of the impact of building form and surface area in which they also consider the insulation values of the fabric elements, giving clues about where insulation needs to be increased as a result of decisions about building form.

CHAPTER 3. THE LOW ENERGY BUILDING ENVELOPE

Heavy buildings heat up and cool down more slowly than light buildings

In a high thermal mass building the rate of change of maximum indoor temperature might be about half of that of the outdoor temperature. Givoni, in *Passive and Low Energy Cooling of Buildings* (1994, p60) has calculated that in a lightweight building, on the other hand, the rate of change of temperature might increase to 0.8 times – in other words, quite closely matching – that of the external temperature. Although each building will vary considerably depending on the construction materials and methods, in high thermal mass buildings there may be a time lag of 10 hours or more between the peak external temperature and the highest internal temperature. Both Olgyay in *Design With Climate, Bioclimatic Approach to Architectural Regionalism* (1963, pp116 and 117) and Thomas in *Environmental Design, an Introduction for Architects and Engineers* (1994, p158) discuss this important principle.

The time lag between maximum outdoor and maximum indoor temperature can be designed to occur at a useful time of night (or day). The Australian Government's *Your Home Technical Manual* (2010 section 4.5) includes a very interesting table indicating the relative thermal lag times of some building materials, concluding that 250mm of concrete would have a thermal time lag of 6.9hrs, 250mm of rammed earth 10.3hrs and 1,000mm of sandy loam a very slow 30 days. In *Ecohouse 2: A Design Guide* (2004, p128), Sue Roaf considers that in a domestic situation each wall inside a house would need to be around 100mm thick to provide sufficient thermal mass to dampen temperature fluctuations and store heat generated within the building.

High thermal mass needs night time ventilation

Research by Givoni to be found in *Passive and Low Energy Cooling of Buildings* (1994, pp60–65) has shown that the maximum internal temperature of a building whose mass is cooled at night might be 3°C (5.4°F) lower than in the same building without the aid of nocturnal cooling. With a maximum outdoor temperature of 36°C (96.8°F) that potentially means a significantly more comfortable 27.5°C (81.5°F) maximum indoor temperature. In arid and desert areas the internal temperature might be 6–8°C (10.8–14.4°F) lower than the outdoor maximum. Openings therefore need to be designed to enable the cool nocturnal air to 'scour' the exposed thermal mass, and Givoni shows us examples of how to maximise the effect of nocturnal ventilation with the design of openings. In climatic regions where high summer daytime temperatures would place the interior outside the comfort zone nocturnal ventilation will be more effective than daytime comfort ventilation.

Thermal mass and insulation

The relation between thermal storage and insulation value is well presented by Yannas in *Solar Energy and Housing Design,* Volume 1 (1994, pp27 and 98). Research carried out in Alaska by Carlson and Siefert, *Building in Alaska – Thermal Properties of Walls* (reprinted 2002) identifies the thermal storage capacities of different wall constructions, confirming the relatively high thermal storage capacity of timber.

Thermal mass and insulation work together

Studies by Kosny et al, in *Thermal Mass – Energy Savings Potential in Residential Buildings* (2001) indicate that, for greatest energy savings, the best location for the insulation layer in a multi-layer wall is central. This confirms a significant body of research suggesting that thermal mass should be in direct contact with the building interior if it is to dampen internal temperature fluctuations. Furthermore, it seems walls with exposed thermal mass might reduce energy needs by almost 10% to 20% over lightweight walls of equivalent insulation value, depending upon climatic location.

Do not forget that heat transfer through a wall will occur irrespective of whether the insulation is on the outside or in the middle of a multi-layer construction – insulation does not completely halt heat flow. In the northern European climate it would be expected today that walls and the ground floor would have 200mm of insulation and roofs 300mm, and that these figures would increase for very cold regions. Haggard et al, in the *Passive Solar Architecture Pocket Reference* (2009, p30) give a useful table of the insulation values needed for roofs and walls in different climatic regions.

When and where to use thermal mass?

The Australian Government's *Your Home Technical Manual* (2010, section 4.9) advises that where diurnal changes of 7–10°C (12.6–18°F) exist thermal mass becomes useful and where diurnal changes are more than 10°C (18°F) then the adoption of thermal mass is 'highly desirable'. The Royal Institute of British Architects in their on-line Sustainability Hub (see Night Ventilation of Thermal Mass) also suggests 5–7 °C (9–12.6°F). Whatever the exact cut-off point, the basic rule is that the greater the diurnal temperature range the higher the quantity of thermal mass needed to dampen temperature changes.

Heavy or light weight – rules for climate

Olgyay, in *Design With Climate, Bioclimatic Approach to Architectural Regionalism* (1963, pp122–124) reminds us that there needs to be a balance between insulation and thermal mass and identifies the ideal locations of thermal mass in different climatic conditions. It is generally the case that in hot-humid locations lightweight construction is preferable but Givoni, as detailed in *Climate Considerations in Building and Urban Design* (1998, p400) has experimented with thermal mass in hot-humid conditions and he concludes that temperature stability will be improved if thermal mass can be employed with effective nocturnal ventilation. Dean Hawkes et al, in *The Selective Environment, An Approach to Environmentally Responsive Architecture* (2002, p39) confirm that homes in cold climates should use thermal mass as a heat store for evening comfort.

Heavy or light weight – rules for occupancy

Pelsmakers, in *The Environmental Design Pocketbook* (2012, p148), states that lightweight buildings without thermal mass should only be proposed for buildings with intermittent use, and holiday homes are cited as an example. A building in constant use is more compatible with a heavyweight construction as heat is retained for use.

What we wear and what we do influences comfort

Acceptable temperature limits for low humidity regions are defined by Givoni in *Climate Considerations in Building and Urban Design* (1998, pp38–39) who proposes 18–25°C (64.4–77°F) in winter and 20–27°C (68–80.6°F) in summer. He also provides a very useful summary (on pp5–22) of the human responses to the thermal environment and confirms that the rate of heat exchange between humans and their internal environment will depend greatly upon clothing and physical activity. Givoni's research confirms that the internal temperature can be significantly lowered without occupant discomfort if people wear more (or more appropriate) clothing. Pelsmakers, in *The Environmental Design Pocketbook* (2012, p136) reminds us that the temperature at the feet should remain at or above 19°C (66.2°F) and that discomfort will be experienced if the temperature at foot level reaches 3°C (5.4°F) lower than at head level. For hot-humid climates Givoni proposes elevating the acceptable upper temperature by 2°C (3.6°F) because people become acclimatized to such conditions. In a fascinating piece of research by the BRE Productive Workplace Centre, Nigel Oseland, in *Adaptive Thermal Comfort Models* (1998, pp41 and 42) defines the temperature benefits of various activities and of putting on or removing various items of clothing: putting on or taking off a collar and tie results in a net temperature benefit of 0.8°K, changing office chair type 0.3°K, consuming a cold drink 0.9°K.

Windows and glass

Glass is an important and complex topic in relation to energy use in buildings: too much glass, or the wrong glass, and poorly placed windows will result in buildings being too hot in summer and too cold in winter. Glass is a poor insulator compared with many other building materials: in winter it readily allows heat from within to escape. A triple-glazed window might halve the heat loss of a double-glazed window, but it takes around 50% more energy (embodied energy) to make a triple-glazed window. It is therefore essential to correctly apply the properties of windows and glass and many authors have covered this topic.

In *The Environmental Design Pocketbook* (2012, pp203 and 204) Pelsmakers discusses thermal performance and compares the performance of double and triple glazing (see p144), in doing so confirming that triple glazing improves thermal comfort in a building because the temperature near to the inner pane is closer to room temperature, limiting surface temperature differences which humans experience as discomfort. In fact, during a very cold winter day, in a room heated to 21°C (69.8°F) the temperature inside close to a high performance double-glazed window might be 16°C (60.8°F) while the near-surface temperature will be 18°C (64.4°F) with a triple-glazed unit. Haggard et al, in the *Passive Solar Architecture Pocket Reference* (2009, p35) consider the different functions of apertures in buildings and discuss the architectural implications. They also usefully tabulate (p36) the thermal and daylighting properties of different window types.

The key properties of glass which are of interest to the low energy designer are:

• Overall U-value, the measure of resistance to heat transfer of the window, including glass and frame. The lower the value the better.

• g-value, or Solar Heat Gain Coefficient (SHGC), the measure of the ability of the window to permit solar gain. The higher the g-value the greater the solar gain will be. A single glazed pane will be best, but will have a poor U-value.

• Low emissivity (low-E), the coating which in cold regions or seasons is used to prevent heat from leaving a room. It can also be employed in hot climates to prevent heat entering a room. The key is which surface of the glass the coating is applied to. The surfaces in a double glazed unit are numbered from the outside to inside, 1, 2, 3 and 4 etc.

• Shading coefficient (SC), a measure, relative to a single-glazed window, of the amount of heat passing through a window. The lower the figure the greater the 'shading'. Beware that often glazing with a low SC is tinted and thus transmits significantly less daylight.

• Daylight transmission value (Tvis), the measure of the amount of daylight transmitted by a window assembly. The higher the value the more daylight will enter the building.

The various properties have to be balanced in relation to the specific climate region and the orientation of the building façades.

Fabric first: insulation, infiltration and windows - the golden rules for retrofit

Because the rules of thumb are universal many apply equally to retrofitting of existing buildings and to new-build projects, and this rule is particularly relevant to retrofitting. Pelsmakers, in *The Environmental Design Pocketbook* (2012 pp229–238) includes a chapter on retrofitting existing housing and considers the payback period for various measures. It is widely acknowledged that the most cost-effective energy-use reduction measure, other than lifestyle change, is to insulate the loft and the cavity wall of a traditionally constructed house in a temperate or cool climate, with a payback period of less than 5 years. Replacing single-glazing with high performance double or triple-glazing will have energy-use benefits (cutting energy bills by up to 40% over single-glazing in cold climates) and the payback period will be 15–30 years.

Heat losses through the fabric of a typical dwelling in a temperate climate – that is a house that has not been specifically designed for minimum energy use – are discussed by Bougdah and Sharples in *Environment, Technology and Sustainability* (2012, pp61–63) and they, and Brian Edwards in *The Rough Guide to Sustainability* (2007 p62) provide a version of the generally acknowledged heat loss percentages through different fabric elements. The Australian Government's *Your Home Technical Manual* (2010, section 4.7) on insulation gives an indication of the heat gains through the same fabric elements in a temperate climate. Remember, materials with a high thermal mass will slow heat flow, but they will not halt it.

Reducing heat loss – earth sheltering

The temperature of the ground under the surface fluctuates with the seasons, but at about 15m depth the ground temperature stabilizes at around the mean annual air temperature which, according to The British Geological Survey, is 8–11°C (46.4–51.8°F) in the UK. This is the origin of the very rough rule of thumb, often quoted in discussions about underground temperatures, which says that the temperature below the surface is 10°C (50°F), and that very general rule is applied in many temperate and hot-summer/cool-winter climate zones. The temperature remains reasonably constant because heat moves very slowly through the high thermal mass of the earth. The reality is that at depths of less than 15m the earth temperature will fluctuate. An article on earth-sheltered homes by Rob Roy, director of the Earthwood Building School, on the website Mother Earth News (October/November 2006) describes building an earth-sheltered home 3m under ground in New York State in the USA. The earth temperature is said to be 4°C (39.2°F) in early March and 16°C (60.8°F) in late August, a useful indication of the beneficial heat and coolth storage capabilities of the earth. Earth-sheltered structures, like green roofs, need to be insulated in most climate regions, to hinder migration of heat from the structure into the surrounding earth. A useful 'climate suitability matrix' may be found in *Sun, Wind and Light: Architectural Design Strategies* (2001, p56) by Brown and DeKay and there is further explanation of the design and operation of earth shelters, with case studies, in *The Green Studio Handbook* by Kwok and Grondzik (2007, pp169–174).

Green roofs, and climate change

From Randall Thomas' *Environmental Design, an Introduction for Architects and Engineers* (2006, p158) there is evidence of a time lag of 12 hours between maximum external and internal temperatures in an office building with a green roof with 500mm of soil, 100mm of insulation on a 150mm concrete slab. If the interior slab is exposed internally then the roof acts both to reduce heat loss and balance temperature changes. A thick green roof is known as intensive whereas shallower depths are also possible and these are known as extensive green roofs. An extensive green roof will only support low-height and resilient planting. Kwok and Grondzik in *The Green Studio Handbook* (2007, p52) note that for small trees 1m of soil depth will be needed, and perhaps 1.8m for large trees. Remember that the additional load of a green roof must be taken into account in structural design.

The UK Environment Agency, in the report, London's Warming: The Impacts of Climate Change updated in May 2012, predicts that summers in 2050 will be between 1.5 and 3.5°C (2.7 and 6.3°F) hotter than today and that the urban heat island effect (UHI), which currently adds 5 to 6°C (9 to 10.8°F) to summer night time temperatures, will strengthen. Coupled with an increased incidence of sudden heavy rainfall and the lack of oxygenating vegetation in our cities, green roofs are seen as one of the means to develop buildings which aim to mitigate the impacts of climate change. Figures from the UK Environment Agency suggest that 4–6 kWh/m²/yr of energy savings can be obtained by using a green roof and this translates as between 7 and 17% of the space heating energy use of a well insulated house.

Reducing heat loss – internal shutters

Yannas, in *Solar Energy and Housing Design*, Volume 1 (1994, p84) calculated the performance of insulated internal shutters and concluded that in a 24 hour period if they were closed for 12 hours they would provide an average U-value (insulation value) equivalent to double glazing. In buildings which have 24 hour occupation (say a home/office) the shutters would have to be designed to admit daylight if day time heat losses were also considered, and this presents an interesting problem for innovative designers to tackle. The effectiveness of heavy curtains is disputed by some, prescribed by others. Hall and Nicholls, in *The Green Building Bible* Volume 2 (2006, p36) propose thick curtains as a substitute for insulated shutters.

CHAPTER 4. ENERGY AND THE INTERNAL ENVIRONMENT

Are we an indoor species?

Dr Nick Baker has written a fascinating paper, 'We are all Outdoor Animals' (on The Daylight Site) in which he reminds us that until quite recently the human species spent most of its time outdoors. Now, according to statistics from the US Environmental Protection Agency in *Buildings and their Impact on the Environment: A Statistical Summary* (2009, p4) we spend more than 90% of our time in buildings, placing obvious demands on energy consumption. More than half of the carbon-derived energy used in a home in a temperate climate is used for space heating, so the sun's power should be harnessed to make a very valuable contribution. The BRE in *Exploiting Sunshine in House Design* (1988, pp53–59) states that for a typical house in a temperate climate increasing the amount of double glazing to a south facing façade will result in only small energy savings, and shading must be used to prevent overheating in summer if the window area exceeds 20% of the wall area. And, as we are reminded by Dean Hawkes et al, in *The Selective Environment, An Approach to Environmentally Responsive Architecture* (2002, p142), passive solar buildings aim to optimise solar-oriented glazing and minimize openings in the opposite façade.

Cold rooms, which are not solar-oriented (north facing in the northern hemisphere) may benefit from direct gains by virtue of a careful manipulation of the section, and north facing windows should be restricted to 10% of the elevation area. The BRE, in *Exploiting Sunshine in House Design* (1988, pp53–59) provides evidence to suggest that in a temperate climate a typical, relatively high mass construction (say masonry) will provide enough thermal mass to dampen diurnal temperature swings by way merely of the internally exposed masonry walls.

Direct, indirect and isolated solar gain

The different ways in which the sun's power may be harnessed in passive solar architecture are described by many authors. Haggard et al, in the *Passive Solar Architecture Pocket Reference* (2009, pp9 and 10) provide handy explanatory diagrams and a brief appraisal of the application and performance of six systems. Hall and Nicholls, in *The Green Building Bible*, Volume 2 (2006, pp39–41) delve further into the complexities of passive solar collectors.

Direct solar gain

In direct solar gain solutions the sun is permitted access into the building, falling on interior surfaces which then re-radiate heat. Thermal mass is usually used in conjunction with direct solar gain and the Australian Government's *Your Home Technical Manual* (2010, Section 4.5) advises that for maximum effectiveness the exposed area of a high thermal mass floor in a direct solar gain design should be around 6 times the area of the window which exposes it to the sun. The orientation of the window is important and should be within about 30° of the midday sun. There is an energy balance for solar gain and heat loss between solar-oriented and non solar-oriented windows. Hall and Nicholls, in *The Green Building Bible,* Volume 2 (2006, pp34–37) rightly conclude that effective solar collecting windows need to have a low U-value (high insulation value) and be capable of being insulated at night (see previous section on internal shutters).

The sunspace

From Brown and DeKay's work, *Sun, Wind and Light: Architectural Design Strategies* (2001, pp171 and 172) we can deduce that in a temperate climate the area of glazing of a south-facing sunspace (north-facing in southern hemisphere) should be between 10% and 20% of the floor area of the building to be heated. With correct orientation (i.e. solar-oriented, or within about 30°) and summer shading a sunspace might, according to various sources including the European research project EASEE: Education of Architects in Solar Energy and Environment, contribute between 15% and 30% to energy savings.

Often a sunspace appears to perform poorly due to lack of understanding, by designers and building users, of how it operates throughout the seasons:

• In summer it needs to be shaded and ventilated to the outside – not open to the inside if hot outdoor air is to be excluded

• On winter days it will act as a buffer zone and, on sunny days, even as a short-term heat source if it is closed to the outside and open to the inside

• On sunny autumn and spring days it will provide much useful heat to adjacent spaces if it is open to indoors and closed to the outside

The presence of thermal mass in the sun space will help in controlling temperature swings and a high performance glass should be used for good insulation values. Performance will be further improved if the sunspace is insulated at night.

Warm air moves towards cool air

This is true whether we are considering outdoor air moving towards indoors or air moving within and between spaces in a building. Haggard et al, in the *Passive Solar Architecture Pocket Reference* (2009, p7) provide a useful chart of the heat sources and sinks which operate in the exchange of energy between people and their environment.

The Trombe wall

The Trombe wall, named after the French engineer Félix Trombe, a pioneer in solar engineering, takes advantage of the fact that glass permits the passage of short wave infra-red radiation which in this case heats a high mass wall behind the glass. The wall works as follows:

• The sun heats the wall

• Heat transfers from the wall, with a time lag, to occupied spaces behind by conduction through the wall

• At the same time a ventilation stack develops between glass and wall due to heated air rising

• Vents allow controlled convection of warm air, without a time lag, from the solar-heated stack into the occupied spaces behind

A Trombe wall needs to be at least 1m high to create an effective stack, according to Hall and Nicholls in *The Green Building Bible,* Volume 2 (2006, p39). They discuss this rule because a constraint which results from the use of Trombe walls is the loss of views, but below-window-sill storage walls are a possible solution. A rule of thumb for the required area of a Trombe wall is difficult to define because the subject is location-sensitive. However, for a house, a figure of 10% of the total floor area (as for glazing area for a sunspace) would be a reasonable starting point and for a 1,000m² two storey building perhaps half that figure.

Some useful guidelines for climatic regions in the United States appear in Brown and DeKay, *Sun, Wind and Light: Architectural Design Strategies* (2001, pp171–175), who confirm that the high mass wall element of the Trombe wall should be 300–400mm thick, or 250–350mm if no vents are introduced. There is no clear rule about the dimension between glass and wall, but in most built examples of Trombe walls the dimension is minimal, enough for construction only. Since the Trombe wall is likely to be built in regions with cold nights the glass outer skin is a source of heat loss and should be insulated at night.

The water wall

Prof. David Bainbridge, in articles published at Motherearthnews.com, provides us with an abundance of first-hand detail on water wall design and construction. He has pointed out that the water wall may also be used for free cooling as long as it is positioned such that breezes may carry the stored coolth into the building and it is he who has given a practical indication of the volume of containers to be used. There are examples of water containers being used as heat/coolth stores in a clerestory, avoiding the problem of view blockage, and such a solution is illustrated in Chapter 5 of this book as a tool for cold climate strategies.

The pond roof

The Skytherm House in Atascadero in California, USA, was the test-bed for this heat storage method. Movable 'bladders' of insulation were devised, making night-time insulation of the heat store possible. Night-time insulation is crucial to avoid heat radiating outwards into the cold night sky rather than being conducted down through the structure, with a time lag, into occupied spaces. The pond roof may also be used for cooling and in this case the pond must be shaded and insulated during the day. Design information may be found in Brown and DeKay, *Sun, Wind and Light: Architectural Design Strategies* (2001, pp176–177). There is a useful review of the main design themes and the available literature by Spanaki titled, *Comparative studies on different type of roof ponds for cooling purposes: literature review,* (2007) and Givoni, in *Passive and Low Energy Cooling of Buildings* (1994, pp152–163) provides detailed scientific study data on roof pond experiments in various locations.

Earth pipes with fluid

This solar energy system relies on the sun having warmed the earth. Coils of pipe are filled with a refrigerant fluid which extracts heat from deep in the ground where temperatures are relatively stable, at around average surface air temperature. A ground source heat pump (GSHP) upgrades the temperature of the fluid into low grade heat, which is adequate for heating water for an underfloor heating system. The heat source might also be used to heat air. Bougdah and Sharples, in *Environment, Technology and Sustainability* (2010, pp113–115) provide a thorough overview of different types of heat pumps and their operation. They define the rule of thumb for length of pipe needed as 30m length for each 1kW of energy to be extracted from the earth. Kwok and Grondzik, in *The Green Studio Handbook, Environmental Strategies for Schematic Design* (2007, pp131–134) examine the design implications of various configurations and set out a sample sizing of a system. Downsides to coil and GSHP systems include the fact that GSHPs are powered by electricity (which might, though, be sourced from the sun) and that only low temperature hot water (at around 40°C [104°F]) can be produced. Too much overlapping or crowding of pipe coils reduces the efficiency of the system because too much heat will be drawn from the earth and the sun might not be able to replenish it over a long period. The efficiency, measured as Coefficient of Performance (COP), of ground source heat pumps is improving each year.

Heat recovery

The idea is to recover heat from rooms which generate it, such as kitchens and bathrooms and to move that heat to rooms which might need it, such as living rooms and bedrooms. Year-round mechanical ventilation with heat recovery (MVHR) should only be adopted for airtight and super-insulated buildings because otherwise air is being exchanged directly with the outside, and this is a premise of the Passivhaus standard of energy efficiency. The standard, which is now being applied in many countries, sets limits in new buildings of:

- space heating energy maximum 15kWh/m^2

- airtightness 0.6 air changes per hour

- fabric U-value maximum 0.15 W/m^2/K

- window U-value maximum 0.8 W/m^2/K

There are also Passivhaus standards for retrofit, known as the Passivhaus: EnerPHit standards and a useful summary of the standards may be found in the *The Environmental Design Pocketbook* by Pelsmakers (2012, pp222 and 223).

Inter-seasonal heat/cool storage

Inter-seasonal storage is not a new idea but there is renewed interest in its potential for low energy solutions in both small scale, single building and large scale district heating applications. A number of working examples exist, including the pioneering Freiburg self-sufficient solar house project by the Fraunhofer Institute for Solar Energy Systems. The house, built in 1992, used a hydrogen-based seasonal heat store and proved that inter-seasonal solar storage could work. In Italy, the University of Calabria in the late 1990s created a successful water-based inter-seasonal store to heat an office building, the water reaching a temperature in October of 70 to 80°C (158 to 176°F) and remaining at a functional temperature through the winter. A summary of these, and other, experiments may be found on the Fujita Research website. Water, if contained in a highly insulated vessel, has benefits over many other storage media, including its large capacity to store heat and its inert physical properties. Pelsmakers, in *The Environmental Design Pocketbook* (2012, p286) considers that 250 litres would be a suitable tank volume for a typical home. Phase-change materials, which store and release energy as they pass from liquid to solid and back, are another medium for inter-seasonal heat storage. A large installation of phase-change materials was adopted by the City of Melbourne for its innovative Council House 2 (CH2) project.

Natural ventilation using wind and bouyancy

It is important to remember that with natural ventilation the internal environment will not be controlled within a narrow comfort band. The CIBSE manual *Natural Ventilation in Non-domestic Buildings* (2011, p4) confirms that temperatures will exceed 25°C (77°F) on occasion. However, with the measures discussed in other sections of this book, such as solar shading, use of thermal mass and nocturnal ventilation, the amount of time a building will exceed thermal comfort conditions will be limited.

Single sided ventilation

In rooms with window openings to one side only the opening acts as both the inlet and outlet for air. Thomas, in *Environmental Design, an Introduction for Architects and Engineers* (2006, p125) is just one author who confirms the rule of thumb that single sided ventilation will work up to a maximum room depth of 6m. Bougdah and Sharples, in *Environment, Technology and Sustainability* (2010, p83) comment on the nature of the window in a single sided ventilation scheme, confirming generations of experience that a window with both high and low openings – such as a traditional vertical sash window – is the most effective for summer ventilation as cool air is drawn in at low level and warm air, rising by stack effect within the room, will be exhausted at high level. A further advantage of high and low level openings is that they will have some effect even during times of still air because the buoyancy of air will create a stack. Givoni, in *Passive and Low Energy Cooling of Buildings* (1994, p46) tells us that if a room has a single window the size of the window will have little impact on the internal airflow, although the impact is greater if the wind is oblique to the wall. Ghiabaklou, in the paper 'Natural Ventilation as a Design Strategy for Energy Saving' (2010, p319), concludes that external vertical fins (wing walls) projecting from one side of the opening will improve the ventilative performance of a window.

Cross ventilation

Cross ventilation will work whether the wind is normal (at 90°) to or obliquely aligned with the façade openings. Some researchers have concluded that cooling by cross ventilation will be most effective if the inlet is smaller than the outlet. Ghiabaklou in *Natural Ventilation as a Design Strategy for Energy Saving* (quoting Sobin, 2010, p317) proposes that the ideal ratio of inlet to outlet is 1: 1.25, and Givoni, in *Passive and Low Energy Cooling of Buildings* (1994, p48) states that such an arrangement provides the highest air speeds. Flow rates will be determined by the smaller of the two openings. There is agreement on the fact that the bigger the openings are the greater the flow and speed of air will be. In *Passive and Low Energy Cooling of Buildings* Givoni (1994, pp26 and 27, and pp 46–49) concludes that because air speeds are higher when the inlet opening is small and the outlet large, such an arrangement might be best suited to rooms such as bedrooms, where the location of desirable cooling is known. Large inlets, on the other hand, lead to better distribution of internal air speeds and so might be best suited to spaces in which people might occupy all parts, such as living spaces. Brown and DeKay, in *Sun, Wind and Light: Architectural Design Strategies* (2001, p65) provide a table which can be used to determine the area of ventilation opening, as a percentage of floor area, related to wind speed and cooling capacity.

Stack ventilation

Air inside a building will commonly be warmer than outside air and the natural buoyancy of warmed air will induce a stack effect. The effectiveness of a stack will be proportional to the square root of temperature difference between top and bottom of the stack. Thomas, in *Environmental Design, an Introduction for Architects and Engineers* (2006, pp125 and 126) ponders the problem that there is a lack of detailed knowledge about stack ventilation, but he provides some guidance on the area of inlets and outlets as a percentage of floor area. In the RIBA's on-line Sustainability Hub, in the section on natural ventilation, Dr Nick Baker provides a useful step-by-step design tool for stack ventilation as well as an in-depth explanation of its operation and application. Solar chimneys, which use the sun's heat to drive a column of air within an enclosed shaft, need to be one storey higher than the top floor to be ventilated.

Cooled earth

Givoni, in *Passive and Low Energy Cooling of Buildings* (1994, pp15–17) experimented with cooled earth solutions and concluded that the difference between outdoor maximum air temperature and the temperature of the cooled earth could be 12–14°C (21.6°–25.2°F) in arid climates and 10–12°C (18–21.6°F) in humid regions. The implication is that the cooler earth provides a sink to cool ventilation air. There are different methods of cooling the earth, shading being the key one. Cooling using water is likely to be restricted to regions and locations with a plentiful local water supply, but given increasing global concerns about water supply and demand this method seems limited in application.

Free cooling – pond roof

Experiments in Mexico by Givoni, detailed in *Passive and Low Energy Cooling of Buildings* (1994, p155) concluded that a pond roof, shaded in daytime with floating insulation, could modify the outdoor maximum temperature by up to 13°C (23.4°F), from an outdoor maximum of 35°C (95°F) to an indoor maximum of 22°C (71.6°F), which compares with an internal temperature of 33°C (91.4°F) without the pond roof. Further information and references may be found earlier in this narrative bibliography, in the section on the pond roof as free a source of heat.

Earth cooling pipes with air

Van Lengen, in *The Barefoot Architect* (2008, pp240–242) considers the use of underground ventilation pipes in dry tropical climates. He suggests using 100mm diameter clay pipes buried at around 2m depth. Givoni, in *Passive and Low Energy Cooling of Buildings* (1994 pp214–218) has experimented with earth cooling tubes and provides much detail on his own and others' work. Van Lengen states that there are no rules for the length of pipes, but although currently information is limited, there are now some emerging rules:

• Bury pipes at least 1.8m deep to take advantage of stable, lower earth temperatures

• Use 100–300mm diameter pipes of a material which is resistant to fungal growth

• There is some evidence that cooling ability peaks at pipe lengths of 50–70 m although hundreds of metres may be needed for larger buildings

• The pipes may be used in reverse to heat incoming air if the soil temperature is higher than desired internal temperature

• Earth pipes are not generally advisable in hot-humid climates due to condensation within the pipes contributing to internal humidity as well as concerns about the pipes harbouring fungal spores

• Earth pipes are unlikely to be cost-effective as the only cooling method due to the extent of pipes and excavation needed

Further information and useful references can also be found at www.builditsolar.com

Sue Roaf et al, in *Ecohouse 2: A Design Guide* (2004, p132) indicate that the air in the earth cooling pipes may be circulated by a fan, which can be powered by a photovoltaic panel.

Using daylight to reduce energy use

The relationship between the amount of daylight available outside and the amount that will be distributed through window openings into a room is known as Daylight Factor (DF). Kwok and Grondzik, in *The Green Studio Handbook, Environmental Strategies for Schematic Design* (2007, pp57–61) discuss the importance of Daylight Factor and although each country has its own standards of daylighting requirements the authors make a suggestion, for design purposes, of the factors which might be aimed at for different building and room types. Thomas, in *Environmental Design, an Introduction for Architects and Engineers* (2006, pp98 and 99) points out that the designer needs to find a balance between the amount of daylight being introduced and the consequences of designing with excessive glazing, such as unwanted heat losses or heat gains. Both Thomas and Kwok and Grondzik re-state the generally understood rule that if a room has a Daylight Factor at the working plane which exceeds 5% the room will appear well daylit but at less than 2% it will seem gloomy. Somewhere in between will result in a daylit room in which the need for artificial light during working hours is minimised.

Window size for sidelighting

Much research points to the fact that the area of a window below the height of the working plane makes little or no contribution to the daylighting of the room. Thomas, in *Environmental Design, an Introduction for Architects and Engineers* (2006, p100) confirms the rule of thumb equation for the relationship between Daylight Factor, room area and window area: average $DF = 20(Ag/Af)\%$, where Ag = area of horizontal glazing, Af = area of floor. If, in order to minimise the times when artificial lighting will be needed we want to achieve a 2.5% Daylight Factor in a domestic living room of $20m^2$ the window area will have to be $2.5m^2$, which would be around 25% of the wall area, slightly more than the overall figure of 20% recommended for low energy performance. This confirms that it is hard to achieve a uniform distribution of an adequate quantity of daylight in a room and that calculation and modelling (either physical with a heliodon and artificial sky and/or by using modelling software such as IES) are needed. However, the rules of thumb provide designers with a sound basis for decision making.

Height of window and depth of room

The problem with daylight is that it diminishes very rapidly as it travels from the window into the depth of a room. Haggard et al, in the *Passive Solar Architecture Pocket Reference* (2009, p67) provide handy sectional diagrams which explain the key means of maximizing the reach of daylight into interior space, which are generally agreed to be:

• Increased ceiling and window height

• Adding a light shelf

• Sloping the ceiling downwards into the room

• High reflectance of internal finishes

Thomas, in *Environmental Design, an Introduction for Architects and Engineers* (2006, p98) also reminds us that tall windows in higher rooms result in a greater throw of light deeper into the room, and greater uniformity in the distribution of daylight. The following equation is commonly used to determine the appropriate relationship between room dimensions and window height: $L/w + L/h \leq 2/(1-Rb)$ where L and w = respectively length and width of the room, h = the window height above the floor and Rb is the weighted reflectance of the room (typically taken to be 0.5). If the left side of the equation is not less than or equal to the right side then the room will be poorly daylit.

Rooflights and light from above

Because lighting levels of about 5,000 lux exist directly overhead on an overcast day it is sensible to consider toplighting where possible, remembering that solar control and heat loss must be managed. Randall Thomas, in *Environmental Design, an Introduction for Architects and Engineers* (2006, p100) states that the average daylight factor for a rooflight is: $DF = 50(Ag/Af)\%$ where Ag = area of horizontal glazing, Af = area of floor. If a daylight factor of 5% is desired in a room of, say, 20m² then the area of the rooflight glazing needs to be 2m². Using the previous rule of thumb equation for sidelighting the same room would need 5m² of glazing and very careful attention to reflectance, colour, room shape and window design, which indicates the significant advantage of rooflights. A wealth of further information relating to many aspects of toplighting, with useful diagrams, can be found in the *Daylighting Guide for Canadian Commercial Buildings* (2002, pp32–38). Pelsmakers, in *The Environmental Design Pocketbook* (2012, p144) proposes a maximum of 12% rooflight area to floor area as a means of limiting heat losses. In hot climates, with high sun angles heat gains are a challenge to be overcome by glazing specification, by limiting rooflight area and by shading.

Haggard et al, in the *Passive Solar Architecture Pocket Reference* (2009, p68) consider the roof monitor, which is a vertical rooflight form commonly adopted as a 'northlight' (in the northern hemisphere) for factories, workshops and studios. They propose, though, to turn it around to face the sun (equator-facing), pointing out that in this orientation the area of glazing can be reduced by up to about 4% of the floor area, and the space can benefit from winter solar heating. A key benefit to opposite-of-equator-facing roof monitors is that they do not admit the sun with its attendant problems of colouration and glare (light which comes from the opposite of the equator is neutral in colour and consistent throughout the day), and so the 'northlight' is favoured by craftsmen and artists. However, credence should be given to the idea of an equator facing, solar controlled roof monitor with modern glazing technology and inventive control of glare and uniformity, especially if useful winter solar heat gains can be harnessed.

Light-coloured interiors, reflectance and window area

White paint will provide a reflectance of 85%, whereas a light grey paint will give 70% and dark carpet 10%. Silver & Mclean, in their *Introduction to Architectural Technology* (2008, p102) state that internal surfaces should have reflectance values of at least 50% for walls, 70% for ceilings and 30% for floors. There is a mathematical relationship between the reflectance of interior surfaces and the window-to-wall (WWR) ratio. When compared with a light room, the WWR will need to be almost double for rooms with dark finishes. A good explanation of this (and other daylighting rules), with some useful diagrams is to be found in the *Daylighting Guide for Canadian Commercial Buildings* (2002, p27). The relationship between room depth and interior reflectance is expressed in the equation $L/w + L/h \leq 2/(1-Rb)$, where L and w = respectively length and width of the room, h = the window height above the floor and Rb = the weighted reflectance of the room. This usually assumes a Rb of 0.5, and if the left side of the equation is less than or equal to 4 then the full depth of a room with windows to one wall will be uniformly daylit.

Exterior colour influences energy use

Givoni, in *Passive and Low Energy Cooling of Buildings* (1994, pp30–33) studies the external colour of a building and its influence on energy use. A reflective, light-coloured building envelope is not only a highly effective but also an inexpensive solar control device, since colour generally involves no extra cost to a project. The effectiveness increases in places with greater diurnal temperature swings, such as would typically be found in arid regions. The colour of a northern façade (south-facing in the southern hemisphere) has little impact on energy consumption in temperate mid-latitude climates, but in regions where the powerful early morning and late afternoon sun reaches the opposite-to-equator-facing elevations colour once again becomes a significant issue.

Olgyay in *Design With Climate, Bioclimatic Approach to Architectural Regionalism* (1963, pp86 and 87) confirms that the roof of a building receives more solar radiation in summer than any other surface, regardless of latitude, making this a significant element in the fabric heat gain equation. The idea of the 'cool roof', which reflects solar energy and reduces cooling needs, is a topic of much current research. Energy savings of at least 10% are possible by incorporating cool roofs in hot climate regions or those with hot summers. The EU Cool Roofs Council rightly points out that there may be a winter heating energy penalty in climates which have hot summers but mild winters, because in achieving summer reflectance the free winter heating capacity of the roof would be lost. This presents the low energy designer with a dilemma. There is therefore also research into building products which can change state – and colour – to vary the solar reflecting/absorbing qualities of roofs and façades depending on the season.

Keeping it simple

In *The Environmental Design Pocketbook* (2012, pp26 and 136) Pelsmakers considers the effect of occupant behaviour on the performance of buildings, and one theme is the intuition which people have towards their environment: it is counter-intuitive in the northern European climate on a hot day to seal a building with closed shutters, windows and doors against heat because we prefer to encourage ventilation. But this would be the correct response. The main theme, though, is that we should ensure our buildings are simple to operate and that users should have control over their environment.

Give clear instructions

A new building will usually have what is known as a maintenance manual, handed to the client upon completion. The manual contains, amongst other things, the instructions and warranties, and repair and maintenance procedures for the equipment and controls built into the project. What is not often provided, however, is a clear operating manual for control of the environment. Without such essential information, written in a form which the users of the building will understand, the ways occupants can manipulate a building to provide comfort with minimal energy inputs will never be learned.

CHAPTER 5. RULES AND STRATEGIES FOR DIFFERENT CLIMATIC REGIONS

As with human comfort, there are different definitions of the world's climate regions and a number of classification systems exist. In general, however, many authors (including Givoni, Bougdah & Sharples, Haggard et al) and teachers in the field of climate-responsive architecture use variations on a simplified version of the widely adopted Köppen climate classification from the 1880s. The simplified climate zones are usually listed as: hot-dry, hot-humid, cold and temperate. Givoni adds a fifth, cold-winter/hot-summer climate zone, which is also explored in this book. Bougdah & Sharples, in *Environment, Technology and Sustainability*

(2010, pp14 and 15) provide a succinct description of the conditions to be found in each climate region, and this differs from Givoni's in *Climate Considerations in Building and Urban Design* (1998, pp333–441). This author therefore gives a précis of the anticipated conditions in each climate zone as they apply to this book, under the climate headings below.

This final chapter sets out the rules of thumb which apply to the different climatic regions, and illustrates architectural strategies in response. All five regions are addressed, with an imagined building acting as a vehicle for investigating each region. Various books have provided information and inspiration for this chapter. Olgyay's important and often quoted work *Design With Climate, Bioclimatic approach to Architectural Regionalism* (1963) introduced the concept of 'bio-climatic' design, a phrase now in common usage. He explained how climate could be studied such that the characteristics beneficial to human comfort and those which are not could be isolated. Hyde, in *Climate Responsive Design* (2000) takes Olgyay's work as a starting point in this very broad-ranging book in which he begins with a useful summary of climate types and characteristics, proceeding to micro-climates, strategies for ventilation and constructional responses to climate issues for, mainly, hot climate regions. Van Lengen's classic green handbook, *The Barefoot Architect* (2008), was first published in 1981 and it contains down-to-earth, practical advice on how to build simple buildings in humid, dry-tropical and temperate climate zones. Beware if you are in the northern hemisphere as van Lengen's diagrams are drawn for the southern hemisphere, so the sun is shown in the north. Givoni's essential 1998 text, *Climate Considerations in Building and Urban Design*, while not intended as a handbook for construction, contains more detail about the specific climatic responses required in each region. Haggard et al in the *Passive Solar Architecture Pocket Reference* (2009, p60) provide a handy summary table of the cooling strategies needed in various climatic regions, referenced to more detailed sections of their pocket book. Bernard Rudofsky's seminal *Architecture Without Architects* (1981, originally published in 1964), which is illustrated with photographs of indigenous or non-pedigree buildings from history provides living proof of the effectiveness of a climate responsive architecture, which has resulted in humans achieving comfort conditions for centuries in a wide range of climates, usually with limited resources.

Hot-dry climate

Found at latitudes between 15 and 30° north and south of the equator, the main focus in this climate region will be on summer cooling but some hot-dry climate zones experience comfortable winters and some can expect very cold winters, so in some cases the winter condition also needs to be addressed, and a heating system might be needed. Givoni, in

Climate Considerations in Building and Urban Design (1998, pp333–342) provides a detailed commentary on this climate region and on the designer's response. Maximum daytime temperatures might reach 50°C (122°F). It is assumed that summer night time ventilative cooling can be achieved because most hot-dry regions experience large diurnal temperature swings with night cooler than day.

Adoption of the strategies indicated in the rules of thumb diagrams could result in maximum summertime indoor temperatures of up to 10°C (18°F) lower than the outdoor maximum. Van Lengen, in *The Barefoot Architect* (2008, pp224–266) provides further information on methods for cooling in hot-dry regions and a particularly informative section on wind towers and wind catchers. Along with shaded courtyards, carefully planned ventilation openings, earth cooling pipes and light colours he identifies further, traditional cooling methods. The windcatcher, an ancient Persian invention, also features in Rudofsky's *Architecture Without Architects* (1981, figs. 113, 114 and 115). The windcatcher works by guiding summer breezes into the shaft at night, for nocturnal cooling. A shutter, or baffle, within the tower is closed during the day to prevent the ingress of hot air. In the winter in hot-dry regions with plentiful sun the scoop faces the sun and the shutter is open during the day to allow in air which has been warmed by the thermal mass of the tower. In winter the shutter is closed at night to prevent heat loss. Further examples and descriptions may be found in Brown and DeKay's *Sun, Wind and Light: Architectural Design Strategies* (2001, pp188–190).

Hot-humid climate

Found at latitudes of 10 to 15 degrees each side of the equator, these climate regions typically experience a fairly constant annual average temperature of around 27°C, with highs of about 30°C (86°F), or more on clear days. High relative humidity (80–90%) is experienced all year and rainfall is also high. Some regions enjoy the trade winds (easterlies) and some are subject to potentially destructive typhoon or hurricane winds.

The preoccupation in this climate is to provide effective ventilation with minimum heating of the building envelope. Haggard et al, in the *Passive Solar Architecture Pocket Reference* (2009, pp61 and 62), while confirming that high humidity makes these most difficult regions in which to provide comfort conditions, particularly in summer, provide us with instructive sectional diagrams explaining ventilation strategies, including for high-rise buildings. Van Lengen, in *The Barefoot Architect* (2008, pp145–147) adds suggestions on the implications on roof form for effective cooling by ventilation. Givoni, in *Climate Considerations in Building and Urban Design* (1998, pp 379–402) dedicates a chapter to hot-humid climate zones and his excellent explanation of the varying characteristics of these regions includes a discussion of the dilemma that in regions with a beneficial, easterly prevailing wind the powerful early morning sun is also in the east and must be intercepted before it enters east-facing windows if overheating is to be avoided and ventilation optimised.

Cold climate

In this book a cold climate is one with cool, comfortable summers and average autumn/winter/spring temperatures of around 0°C (32°F), and this follows Givoni's definition in *Climate Considerations in Building and Urban Design* (1998, p417). In these climatic regions the designer's focus is on reducing the need for heating energy in the winter, and a significant influence on winter temperatures is wind chill. Bougdah and Sharples, in *Environment, Technology and Sustainability* (2010, p14) group cold and polar climate regions, in which average winter temperatures might be -15°C (5°F) or below. Givoni, in *Climate Considerations in Building and Urban Design* (1998, pp417–430) addresses the cold climate at both the building and urban scale and makes reference to super-insulation and to direct solar gain, emphasising the importance of orientation. These are factors which apply in both cold and polar conditions, and the rules of thumb work for both too.

Cold-winter/hot-summer climate

There are places which experience cold or very cold winter conditions and warm or hot and humid summer conditions, and these need to be treated differently from the merely hot or cold regions. The cold-winter/hot-summer climate regions currently occur on, and inland of, the eastern seaboards of China, Japan and the USA and also in many continental locations on earth, where the tempering influence of the sea does not exist. Givoni in *Climate Considerations in Building and Urban Design* (1998, pp431–441) examines this distinct climate type and, as with the other regions, provides us with building and urban design considerations. Givoni also proposes the notion of a changing building form which could provide an increased envelope for cooling in summer and a reduced, compact form in winter.

Temperate climate

Van Lengen, in The *Barefoot Architect* (2008, pp270–293) considers the temperate climate region as one in which the goals are to keep heat out in summer and prevent heat loss in winter. In other words, the designer's focus is to reduce winter heating needs and prevent overheating in summer, and this is confirmed in a useful comparison table by Hyde in *Climate Responsive Design* (2000, p57). The result is that many of the rules of thumb come together in a strategy which also takes advantage of free heating in winter and buffers living spaces against cold winds and lack of sun. Van Lengen in *The Barefoot Architect* (2008, p279) introduces a fireplace into his temperate climate strategies, and as long as there is a sustainable source of fuel, and airtightness is not a primary goal, this seems a sensible provision. Haggard et al, in the *Passive Solar Architecture Pocket Reference* (2009, pp58 and 59) provide information about glazing areas and areas for thermal mass in temperate (and other) climatic regions in their consideration of passive heating.

Bibliography

• Bougdah, H., and Sharples, S., (2010). *Environment, Technology and Sustainability*. Taylor & Francis. Abingdon.

• Brown, G. Z., and DeKay, M., (2001). *Sun, Wind and Light : Architectural Design Strategies*. Wiley, New York.

• Building Research Establishment (prepared by Eclipse Research Consultants), (1988). *Exploiting Sunshine in House Design*. BRE, Watford. www.eclipseresearch.co.uk/download/energy/Solar-handbook.pdf

• Building Research Establishment, (April 1990). BRE Digest 350, *Climate and Site Development* Part 3: BRE, Watford.

• CIBSE, (1999). *Daylighting and window design: Lighting Guide* LG10. CIBSE, London.

• CIBSE, (2011). *Natural Ventilation in non-domestic buildings*. CIBSE Applications Manual AM10. CIBSE, London.

• Edwards, B., (2010). *The Rough Guide to Sustainability*. RIBA Publishing. London.

• Givoni, B., (1994). *Passive and Low Energy Cooling of Buildings*. Wiley, New York.

• Givoni, B., (1998). *Climate Considerations in Building and Urban Design.* Wiley, New York.

• Haggard, K., Bainbridge, D., ALijilani, R. (Goswami, D. Y. ed)., (2009). *Passive Solar Architecture Pocket Reference*. Earthscan, Germany.

• Hall, K., and Nicholls, R., (2006). *The Green Building Bible Volume 2.* Green Building Press, Llandysul.

• Hawkes, D., McDonald, J., and Steemers, K., (2002). *The Selective Environment, An Approach to Environmentally Responsive Architecture*. Spon, London.

• Henson, R., (2007). *The Rough Guide to Weather*. Rough Guides, London.

• Humphreys, M., (1995) *Thermal Comfort Temperatures and the Habits of Hobbits*. Contained in: Nicol, F., Humphreys, M., Sykes, O., and Roaf, S., (editors), (1995). *Standards for Thermal Comfort: Indoor Air Temperature Standards for the 21st Century*, Spon, London.

• Hyde, R., (2000). *Climate Responsive Design*. Taylor and Francis, New York.

• Kwok, A., G., and Grondzik, W., T., (2007). *The Green Studio Handbook, Environmental Strategies for Schematic Design*. Architectural Press, Oxford

• Levy, M., (2007). *Why the Wind Blows – A History of Weather and Global Warming*. Upper Access, Hinesburg.

• Littlefair, P. J., Santamouris, M., Alvarez, S., Dupagne, A., Hall, D., Teller, J., Coronel, J. F. and Papanikolaou, N., (2000). *Environmental Site Layout Planning: Solar Access, Microclimate and Passive Cooling in Urban Areas*, HIS/BRE Press, Watford.

• Olgyay, V. (1963) *Design With Climate, Bioclimatic Approach to Architectural Regionalism*. Princeton University Press, Princeton.

• Oseland, N., (1998). Adaptive thermal comfort models. Published in *Building Services Journa*l, December 1998, pp41 and 42.

• Pelsmakers, S., (2012). *The Environmental Design Pocketbook*. RIBA Publishing, London.

• Roaf, S., Fuentes, M., and Thomas, S.,(Second edition, 2004). *Ecohouse 2: A Design Guide*. Architectural Press, Oxford.

• Rudofsky, B. (1981). *Architecture Without Architects: A Short Introduction to Non-Pedigreed Architecture* (5th impression). Academy Editions, London

• Silver, P., and McLean, W., (2008). *Introduction to Architectural Technology*. Laurence King, London.

• Thomas, R. (2006). *Environmental Design, an Introduction for Architects and Engineers*. Taylor and Francis, New York.

• Van Lengen, J. (2008). *The Barefoot Architect*. Shelter Publications Inc., Bolinas, California.

• Yannas, S., (1994) *Solar Energy and Housing Design*, Volume 1. Architectural Association Publications, London

Web-based resources:

• Bainbridge, D. A. (1983). Build a Water Wall Home. www.motherearthnews.com/Green-Homes/1983-11-01/Build-a-Water-Wall-Home.aspx

• Baker, N., We are all outdoor animals.
www.thedaylightsite.com/showarticle.asp?id=38&tp=6

• British Geological Survey – ground temperature.
www.bgs.ac.uk/reference/gshp/gshp_report.html

• www.builditsolar.com

• Carlson, A., and Siefert, R. D. (2002). *Building in Alaska – Thermal Properties of Walls*. University of Alaska Fairbanks EEM-04756.
icecubetopper.com/pdfs/docs/ak/u_ak/freepubs/EEM-04756.pdf

• Chappell, H., and Shove, E., (2004). *Comfort: A review of philosophies and paradigms*.
www.lancs.ac.uk/fass/projects/futcom/fc_litfinal1.pdf.

• Council House 2.
www.melbourne.vic.gov.au/Environment/CH2/aboutch2/Pages/CoolingSystem.aspx#Chilled

• *Daylighting Guide for Canadian Commercial Buildings*.
www.enermodal.com/pdf/DaylightingGuideforCanadianBuildingsFinal6.pdf

• Compact form. Article in Issue 36. /oikos.com/esb/36/bldgform.html

• EASEE: Education of Architects in Solar Energy and Environment.
www-cenerg.ensmp.fr/ease/sunspace_overheads.pdf

• EU Cool Roofs Council. www.coolroofs-eu.eu/

• Freiburg self-sufficient solar house, Fraunhofer Institute for Solar Energy Systems. www.ise.fraunhofer.de/en/areas-of-business-and-market-areas/copy_of_hydrogen-technology/hydrogen-generation-and-storage/electrolysis/energy-self-sufficient-solar-house

• Fujita Research. www.fujitaresearch.com/reports/solarpower.html

• www.gaisma.com

• Ghiabaklou, Z., (2010). *Natural Ventilation as a Design Strategy for Energy Saving*. World Academy of Science, Engineering and Technology 71, pp315 - 320. www.waset.org/journals/waset/v71/v71-56.pdf

• www.iesve.com

• www.jaloxa.eu

• Kosny, J., Petrie, T., Gawin, D., Childs, P., Desjarlais, A., and Christian, J. (2001, updated by Diane McKnight). *Thermal Mass* - Energy Savings Potential in Residential Buildings. Buildings Technology Center, Oak Ridge National Labs and Polish Academy of Sciences.
www.orln.gov/sci/roofs+walls/research/detailed_papers/thermal/index.html

• www.passivhaus.org.uk

• Public Works and Government Services Canada. (2002).
www.enermodal.com/pdf/DaylightingGuideforCanadianBuildingsFinal6.pdf

• Quam, V., Wight, B. and Hirning, H., (1993, reviewed and reprinted 1996). *Farmstead windbreaks*. North Dakota State University. www.ag.ndsu.edu/pubs/plantsci/trees/f1055w.htm

• RIBA Sustainability Hub. www.architecture.com/SustainabilityHub/SustainabilityHub.aspx

• Roy, R., (2006). *Earth-sheltered homes*. www.motherearthnews.com/Green-Homes/2006-10-01/Earth-sheltered-Homes.aspx#ixzz1nr7ecACt

• Spanaki, A., (2007). Comparative studies on different type of roof ponds for cooling purposes, literature review1009 2nd PALENC Conference and 28th AIVC Conference on Building Low Energy Cooling and Advanced Ventilation Technologies in the 21st Century, September 2007, Crete. www.inive.org/members_area/medias/pdf/Inive/PalencAIVC2007/Volume2/PalencAIVC2007_V2_084.pdf

• UK Environment Agency, London's Warming: The Impacts of Climate Change. www.environment-agency.gov.uk/business/sectors/91970.aspx

• United States Department of Agriculture, Natural Resources Conversation Service. Conservation Practices that Save: Windbreaks/Shelterbelts. Plant-materials.nrcs.usda.gov/technical/publications/windbreak-pubs.html (see also: www.nrcs.usda.gov/wps/portal/nrcs/detailfull/national/energy/?&cid=nrcs143_023634)

• United States Environmental Protection Agency (2009). *Buildings and their Impact on the Environment: A Statistical Summary* (Revised April 22, 2009). www.epa.gov/greenbuilding/pubs/gbstats.pdf

• Your Home Australian Government technical manuals. www.yourhome.gov.au